THE KYLES

(na Caol)

a celebration of 100 years

edited by

IAIN THORBURN

First Published 1996
Argyll Publishing
Glendaruel
Argyll PA22 3AE
Scotland

British Library Cataloguing-in-Publication Data.
A catalogue record for this book is available from the British Library.

ISBN 1 874640 27 0

Origination
Cordfall Ltd, Glasgow

Printing
Bookcraft (Bath) Ltd

Kyles Athletic
would like to acknowledge
the support of the following:

Argyll & Bute District Council,
Hydro Electric Community Fund Scheme,
Royal Bank of Scotland plc, A&A Macrae & Sons,
Neil Blair & Sons, N Ferguson, Kyles of Bute Hotel,
County Garage Dunoon, James Watt College, Dr JG Paterson,
Ormidale Management Development Centre,
D&P MacPhail, Lighthouse of Scotland, Black of Dunoon,
Blacks Transport, CM Black, MM Cameron, Gaelic Partnership,
Andrew Irvine & Son, Royal Hotel Tighnabruaich,
the McBride family, Mr & Mrs E Williams, David Gieve,
J Campbell Glen Caladh, Dr David Lockie, the Jamieson family,
Ballimore Estate, Gibsons of Dunoon, the Stevenson family,
Otter Ferry Salmon Ltd, Stewart McNee (Dunoon) Ltd,
Fyfe Ireland WS Solicitors, Edinburgh
Altered Image Hairdressers, Ferguslie Garage Sandbank,
N&A Macdonald, Kyles of Bute Salmon, Peter Scott
and the many other people
who paid for subscription copies of the book.

Kyles Athletic Shinty and Football Club 1896/7 when the club colours
were red and white hoops
Committee (l to r): Piper McFarlane, R McLean, D Weir, J McLachlan,
*   W Douglas, J Black, W Brown, H Hazell (treasurer),*
*   DT Colquhoun (president)*
middle: T Nicolson, A Jamieson, J Benn, A Gemmell, G Duncan, A Benn,
*   H Nicolson*
front: N White, J Weir, N Nicolson, J McNeill (captain), R Scott

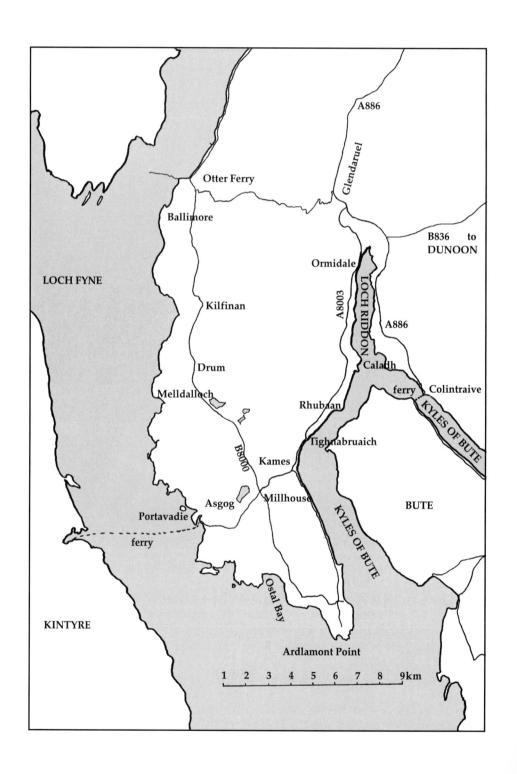

A886

Glendaruel

Otter Ferry

Ballimore

B836 to
DUNOON

Ormidale

LOCH FYNE

Kilfinan

A8003

LOCH RIDDON

A886

Drum

Caladh

Melldalloch

ferry

Colintraive

Rhubaan

KYLES OF BUTE

Tighnabruaich

B8000

Kames

Asgog

Millhouse

BUTE

Portavadie

ferry

KYLES OF BUTE

Ostal Bay

KINTYRE

Ardlamont Point

1   2   3   4   5   6   7   8   9km

CONTENTS

LIST OF ILLUSTRATIONS

RO-RADH

Fàilte gu Leabhar nan Ceud Bliadhna Buidheann Camanachd nan Caol agus mòran taing airson pàirt a ghabhail anns na cuimhneachain urramach againn.

Bhon chiad choinneimh de Chomataidh Bliadhna na Ceud tha sinn air a bhith a'tuairmeachadh air eachdraidh na Buidhne a chomharrachadh ann an clò-bhualadh. Tha an leabhar seo a'toirt iomradh air ceud bliadhna de Bhuidheann Camanachd nan Caol, agus tha mi cinnteach gu meas sibh obair luachmhor agus rannsachadh an sgiobaidh a thug seo am fianais. Chan eil leabhar sam bith comasach air làn-iomradh na Buidhe agus na sgìre fhoillseachadh, ach caisgidh e iomadach argamaid agus 's dòcha gun tòisich e connspaid no dhà as ùr.

Bho thàinig camanachd eagaraichte gu bith tha Buidheann nan Caol air a bhith a'dèanamh làn-oidhirp air taic a thoirt don gheam a chumail a'dol, mu thimcheall nan Caol Bhòdach agus ann an coimhearsnachdan eile. Air sgàth sin tha camanchd air an sgìre dhuaiseachadh le dearbh-aithne agus inbhe nach eil faicsinneach ro thric ann an coimhearsnachdan dùthchail an latha'n diugh. Bho thòiseachadh beag tha Buidheann nan Caol air a dhol air adhart gu bith 'na prìomh bhuidheann anns an Sgìre a Deas, a'cosnadh fichead duais anns a' Chupa Camanachd; anns an dàrna h-àite a-mhàin ri ar prìomh cho-dheuchainne Bail' Ur an t-Slèibh.

Tha e a'cur moit orm a bhith 'nam cheann-suidhe air a'Bhuidheann rè Bliadhna nan Ceud agus is e urram mhòr a th'ann a bhith a'leantainn cinn-suidhe à teaghlaichean-camanachd ainmeil mar Clann 'Ic Neacail, Clann 'Ic Rath, Clann 'Ic Phàdraig, Clann 'Ic Shimidh agus Clann 'Ic Creamhain. Tha cuimhneachain mhìorbhaileach againn uile air buinigidhean, briseadh-dùil, càirdeas, fealla-dhà agus a'tarraing mar sgioba, feadhainn dhiubh a bhios air an ath-bheothachadh anns na duilleagan seo. Tha mi a'guidhe deagh shealbh agus a'rùnachadh gu lean a'Bhuidheann oirre gu làidir soirbheachail airson iomadh bliadhna eile.

John Paterson
Club President 1996

FOREWORD

Welcome to Kyles Athletic's Centenary Book and thank you for joining our celebrations.

From the first meeting of the Centenary Committee, a publication to mark our history has been one of our main ventures. This book plots one hundred years of Kyles Athletic Shinty Club and I am sure you will find all the hard work and research by the enthusiastic production team has been worthwhile. No book will tell the whole story of the club and district but it will settle many arguments and may even start a few new ones.

Since organised shinty began, Kyles Athletic have participated fully to support and sustain the game around the Kyles of Bute and beyond. Shinty in turn has rewarded the district with a focus and identity not always obvious in present-day rural communities. From a small beginning, the Kyles have gone on to be the top club in the South Area with twenty wins in the Camanachd cup – a total second only to our main rivals Newtonmore.

It is a privilege to be the president of the club during its centenary and a great honour to follow presidents from such famous shinty families as the Nicolsons, Macraes, Patersons, Jamiesons and Crawfords. We all have wonderful memories of achievements, disappointments, friendships, fun and teamwork, some of which will be re-kindled in these pages. Here's to many more and to the continuation of a thriving and successful club!

John A Paterson
Club President 1996

The Kyles had been well-known as a sailing centre from the arrival of the age of steam. Pictures show sailing in the Kyles in the 1990s (top); in the 1960s (right) and (bottom, left) sailors and (bottom, right) SY **Iolande** *at Tighnabruaich Regatta in the 1950s*

Kyles Athletic Shinty Club is one hundred years old this year. While it would be difficult to overstate the club's contribution to the community's sense of identity – for a start, there are thousands of people in Scotland who might not have heard of Tighnabruaich were it not for the success of The Kyles – we have taken the opportunity to record some of the events of the past century, and beyond, which have shaped that community as well as the club.

It is more than ten years since the Ardlamont Preservation Society and the Kyles of Bute Improvements Trust produced their last publications on the district's past and present. Both of these had chapters on shinty. In this book we have reversed the balance between shinty and its local cultural and historical background.

We have also sought to place shinty in its wider sporting context – the club was originally Kyles Athletic Shinty and Football Club. Unlike Vale of Leven, which excelled in both shinty and football for a time, Kyles seem to have dropped football early, just as the Vale eventually dropped shinty. Athletics remained important for Kyles until the Second World War, and the Nicolsons of Kyles dominated heavy athletics throughout that period. T R Nicolson was an Olympian. In sailing, Duncan 'Bunks' Currie competed in the Americas Cup. You cannot go higher. We have recorded these facts in part to counteract the patronising attitude towards shinty so often adopted by commentators on 'majority' sports, who see nothing but admirable blood and guts. We know that shinty is more than just a game. But we also know that shinty players are athletes and sportsmen.

The Kyles of Bute were, of course, famous long before Kyles Athletic arrived on the scene – as our MacBrayne's extract shows. And thanks to the Tighnabruaich Town Regatta, the district had been on one sporting map for more than fifty years. The regatta may not be what it was, but outside of the Highlands, the Kyles are still more likely to be associated with water sports than with shinty.

As with much of the Highlands, the district was opened up by the steam age – which brought steamers where other areas got trains. It was sea transport that brought industrialisation – in the shape of the Powderworks at Millhouse and Kames – and holiday-makers. And transport is a major theme in the history of Kyles Athletic.

As for most clubs, until World War II, the great majority of the competitions were local and junior. The sense of isolation and distance survived the War, as the papers of the Schools Camanachd Association can attest. And even in 1994, travel difficulties were not insignificant in the decision of the players not to take up their place in the National League.

But, to go back to 1896 the estates and farms, from Otter Ferry to Ardlamont to Caladh remained big employers. And families were large. Farmers, yachtsmen, and boatbuilders had one thing in common – a busy summer, and spare time in winter. The winter pastimes were curling and shinty. That, and the late Victorian passion for organising and codifying sport, is what brought Kyles Athletic into being.

In the club's first fifty years play was interrupted by two World Wars. In addition, there were not in those days the number of competitions – not to mention leagues – that we find today. So the great Kyles teams of this era would play far fewer games in a season than their modern counterparts. Indeed, since the competitions were knock-out, a bad season might comprise less than half-a-dozen games. Most of the shinty played then, as Douglas MacFie's contribution from Bute confirms, was at junior level – and much of that, especially in the early years, was made up of bounce games.

This background perhaps makes Kyles' achievements in the first ten years of this century even more impressive. They burst on to the north stage in 1904, with a 4-1 victory against Laggan at Kingussie, and followed up with successive wins against Newtonmore – the team which was to end this run and start an even more successful series of their own.

The introduction of the Sutherland Cup in 1923 was timely and

Carts at the shore at Kames, thought to be awaiting the unloading of coal from a puffer in the early years of the century

Shipping mails at Tighnabruaich pier – the 19th century steam age gave a fillip to the local economy

Early century scenes in the Kyles

Herring gutters

Smith's boatshed, Tighnabruaich built a variety of small craft

Deliveries from the pier shop

Tighnabruaich pier traffic 1948

*Apart from servicing the needs of Victorian
visitors, the main summer employment was
on the estates, fishing and farming. Winter
saw longer leisure hours for sports like
curling and shinty*

important. Bute lost 3-2 to Newtonmore in the first final; Kyles beat Newtonmore by the same score in the second. Indeed Kyles' four Sutherland Cup wins before the war, and the four since, are worthy of as much celebration as any of the senior team's Camanachd successes. The junior cup must have been the more difficult to win, particularly before the Balliemore Cup became the competition for Division II teams and the Sutherland for second teams.

We could have filled many pages with anecdotes about games involving Kilfinan, Millhouse, Kames, Tighnabruaich, Glendaruel and Colintraive, but unfortunately the shinty clubs of the district – and Tighnabruaich was formed in 1879 at the latest – did not set the same store as the Curling Club on the keeping of records.

The same could be said of Kyles, the club which is the subject of this publication.

In 1873 a meeting of the Kilfinan Parish School Board decided that the schools at Ardlamont, Otter Ferry and Kilfinan were adequate to the needs of 30, 23 and 68 5–13 year-olds respectively. Millhouse, with 144, had two schools, sited too far away from the centre, and 'insufficient'.

Tighnabruaich had 156, and a school that was wholly inadequate. And so the Board resolved to build new schools at Millhouse and Tighnabruaich in 1877. Today there is one primary school, with a roll of about sixty.

The Millhouse-Kames Powderworks started operation in 1839. Materials were imported by sea, via the works' own pier at Kames, and the gunpowder was exported by the same method. In the earliest days the cargoes were carried by sailing ships, but the trade was taken over by Puffers. Deep sea vessels anchored near the Bute shore, and the gunpowder barrels taken to them in smaller boats. Kames had a factory where saltpetre was refined, before being take to Millhouse for processing by machinery driven by water turbines. During the First World War two steam engines were installed, fuelled by coal imported via Kames.

Serious explosions, in which workers were killed, occurred in 1842, 1846, 1863 and 1870. The last fatality resulted from a burning accident when the machinery in the High Mill Corning House was

The 1920s saw the Kyles established as a serious force in shinty –
above are the men of the Kyles who swept all before them in 1920 when
they won all available trophies

Action from the 1928 Camanachd Cup Final played in Glasgow against Boleskin – Kyles won 6–2.
During that decade they won the Camanachd Cup five times

being dismantled in 1922. The works had closed in 1921, with the loss of sixty jobs.

Yet it was in this decade that Kyles consolidated their position in the game, winning the Camanachd Cup in 1920, 22, 24, 27, and 28; the Sutherland Cup in 1924; and the Celtic Cup in 1920, 21, 22, 23, 27, 28 and 29. The most remarkable of these victories was in 1927, when Kyles won 2-1 after extra time against a team that was called Newtonmore but was in fact a Badenoch select. Kingussie had beaten Kyles in the 1921 final, but they and Newtonmore both felt success was eluding them and decided to amalgamate for two years – to beat the Kyles, we reckoned.

'The Team o' the North' met the following Kyles team at Inverness on April 9, 1927: Donald MacFadyen, John Kennedy, Hugh Henderson, Alex Malcolm, Alan MacFadyen, Malcolm Nicolson, Donald Kent, Archie Weir, Donald Macrae, Andrew Nicolson, Willie Mackenzie, and Willie Greenshields. There was no scoring at full-time, and 'Newtonmore' opened the scoring in extra time. Alan MacFadyen quickly equalised, and with minutes left, Willie Greenshields scored the winner. The Captain was Donald Macrae, whose son Alistair (Wull), captained the cup-winning Kyles team of 1962. This is a unique 'double' for the club, and perhaps even for the game at large. Unfortunately, neither of Wull's sons, Donald and Iain won the Camanachd as captain.

The thirties, by contrast, saw only one Camanchd win, in 1935, but Sutherland success in 1931, 32, and 35; Celtic wins in 1933 and 39; and the Dunn Cup in 1938.

Curling continued to thrive, as did golf, sailing and athletics. The regatta and the Kyles sports were held in Rhubaan every summer. And dances held in connection with these events – as with the shinty and golf clubs – were highlights of the summer season.

But in the twenties and thirties the main 'industrial' development (also seasonal) was in fishing when the 'Klondikers' would fill the Kyles, as large steam vessels sought to buy herring from the small smacks. Up to a hundred fisher-lassies, many of them from the North-East, were employed gutting and salting the fish – at the factory and pier of the former powderworks.

21

When War came it brought evacuees, Italian prisoners, and British and American troops who used Ardlamont and much of Millhouse to practise for the invasion of Europe. Their explosives caused as much damage in the district in one year as the Gunpowder Works accidents in almost a century. But they left us the Tank Slip, and failed to destroy Ostal Bay.

Auchenlochan Pier still very much in use in 1948

Fish farming Kyles shinty players of the 1990s
(l to r) Roddie MacColl, Sean Mobeck, Neil Nicolson, Peter Mobeck

THE KYLES

WHITE APRON DAYS

The significance of 'White Apron' days comes from the time when Kyles had a victory, Peter McCallum of the Post Office at Millhouse would come to the door of his shop and wave his apron.

1896 First Camanachd Cup final; first modern Olympics held in Athens; Nobel Prize established, Klondyke gold rush begins, Niagara Falls Hydroelectric plant opened, Kyles Athletic formed.

1898 Kyles enter Camanachd Cup.

1904 Kyles 4, Laggan 1, at Kingussie. Marlene Dietrich born, Licensing Laws introduced, immigrant fare to USA $10, Olympic Games, St Louis.

1905 Kyles 2, Newtonmore 0, at Inverness. Einstein formulates General Law of Relativity, Russia loses Japanese war, sailors mutiny on battleship Potemkin.

1906 Kyles 4, Newtonmore 2, at Inverness. HMS Dreadnought launched, San Francisco earthquake, Olympic Games, Athens.

1907 Newtonmore 7 Kyles 2, Newtonmore keep trophy till 1911, Kyles lost two in a row, 1913 and 14 to Beauly and Kingussie.

Tally to World War I
Camanachd Cup wins –
Kingussie 5; Newtonmore 4; Kyles, Ballachulish, Beauly 3
Celtic Cup – Kyles had 3 wins – 1901, 1903, 1910.

1920 Kyles 2 Kingussie 1, Glasgow after 0-0 at Inverness. Joan of Arc canonised, Sugar Ray Robinson born, Tommy gun patented, Olympic Games in Antwerp.

1921 Kingussie reverse result, Millhouse/Kames Powderworks close with loss of 60 jobs. Not a white apron year.

1922 Kyles 6, Beauly 2 at Oban. BBC (2LO) opens, new tennis White Apron Days stadium at Wimbledon, *Readers Digest* founded.

1924 Kyles 2, Newtonmore 1 at Kingusssie (after 3-3, Glasgow). Lenin dies, Gandhi fasts Hitler jailed, Rocky Marciano born, All Blacks undefeated tour of Britain, *Chariots of Fire* Olympics, Paris.

1927 Kyles 2, Newtonmore 1 at Inverness. *The Jazz Singer*, Al Jolson (first talkie), Lindbergh flies Atlantic, 15 millionth Model T Ford produced, Hitler's Nazi manifesto published.

1928 Kyles 6, Boleskine 2 at Glasgow. Earl Haig dies, DH Lawrence's *Lady Chatterley's Lover* and the first Mickey Mouse films, Fleming discovers penicillin, Amsterdam Olympics.

1929 Newtonmore 5, Kyles 3 at Spean Bridge.

1934 Caberfeidh 3, Kyles 0 at Inveraray.

1935 Kyles 6, Caberfeidh 4 at Inverness. Luftwaffe formed, Hitchcock's *The 39 Steps*, Malcolm Campbell's Bluebird does 276.8 mph

1936 Newtonmore 1, Kyles 0 at Spean Bridge, after 2-2 at Oban.

1939 Caberfeidh 2, Kyles 1 at Inverness.

Tally to World War II
    Kyles 9, Newtonmore 8, Kingussie 6 Camanachd wins.
    Celtic Cup wins, 1920, 21, 22. 23. 27, 28, 29, 33, 39.
    Sutherland Cup, 1924, 31, 32, 35.
    Dunn Cup, 1938

IN THE BEGINNING

WHAT IT MIGHT HAVE BEEN LIKE

Ronnie MacFarlane

The wind blew and the rain lashed against the windows of the solid stonebuilt farmhouse. The century had but four years to run as five men gathered solemnly round the long deal table in front of the glowing fire in the kitchen range. Their purpose – to form a shinty team to respresent the district in the grand old Scottish game.

At the head of the table sat the massive bearded figure of Neil Nicolson, a giant of a man who had been no mean wielder of the caman in his younger days. On his right sat Arthur Barratt the Tighnabruaich dominie – a spare, dapper man whose immaculate winged collar, tie, and gold stick pin lent an air of distinction to the scene.

On his left was George Irvine – the local draper – a man much respected in the community not only for his business acumen but also for his musical ability. George's features – adorned with a smart military-type moustache – had an almost patrician-like quality, giving him a distinct air of authority. Next to George sat Walter Brown – 'Wattie' – small and bronzed, his weather-beaten features were evidence of his trade of fisherman on the skiff *Watchful*. The *Watchful* plied its trade by buying herring from the fleets which scoured the waters of Argyll for the silver darlings. A canny man, Wattie provided the basic common touch so essential for the success of any body of men charged with the creation of a sporting unit likely to reflect credit on the community they were formed to represent.

27

The group was completed by the figure of D T Colquhoun – the Millhouse dominie ranged alongside his fellow dispenser of the tawse.

They formed an incongruous contrast those two practitioners of learning: Barratt quick and fiery in temperament and Colquhoun, a bigger man with, in today's terms, a laid-back approach. Each complemented the other and their success could be measured by the number of pupils who went on to distinguished careers.

In the absence of recorded tapes, or even written minutes, we can but speculate on the deliberations which took place on that stormy night. However, I think it is safe to assume that while Nicolson was undoubtedly the driving force, Irvine would be concerned with the financial side. The two schoolmasters would be responsible for the Club being operated along clearly defined lines. And Wattie's commonsense approach would undoubtedly be the cement which bound the whole committee together.

With such solid foundation, is it any wonder that as the Kyles Athletic Shinty Club reaches its centenary, not only is it held in high esteem in the shinty world, but its name continues to appear on the trophies available for competition?

And what of the future? The administrative basis, the tradition, the playing standards, and the community support are well and truly in place. The only cloud on the horizon has nothing to do with shinty It rests on the falling levels of population in the feeder areas on which the Club is dependent for future wearers of the Royal Blue.

However, there is little doubt that the spirit that has inspired Kyles teams in the past will continue to do so and that the blue ribbons will continue to grace the Camanachd Cup throughout the next century.

Mr & Mrs Andrew Irvine, founder of Andrew Irvine and Son and parents of Andrew George Irvine, one of the founders of Kyles Athletic

The Irvines

A commonplace sight on the roads of Argyll for many a long year is of large vans bearing the name 'Andrew Irvine & Son, Tighnabruaich'. No history of shinty in the Kyles would be complete without some reference being made to this old family firm of drapers and clothiers first established in 1857 – some thirty-nine years before the shinty club came into existence.

Over the years the Irvine family have had a close relationship with Kyles Athletic, dating back to that original meeting when Andrew George Irvine sat in on that original meeting which led to the formation of the club. Since that inaugural meeting the family have served the club in many capacities – both administrative and over the years with distinction on the field of play.

Like the club, the firm has come a long way since it was first founded. The modern fully equipped vans which bear the Irvine name, for example, are a far cry from the much more primitive forms of transport used in the mid-nineteenth century. Starting off with pedal cycles, they moved on to motorbikes (with sidecars to carry the goods), then to light vans.

Like the shinty club, Irvine's have retained the connection with their roots – the present day management being in the hands of the founder's great-great-grandsons, a truly remarkable feature in these times of great change. And it could be that, with another generation 'in the wings' yet more Irvines will pull on the Royal Blue jersey of the Kyles and carry on the proud tradition.

Ronnie MacFarlane

Alistair Irvine

Irvine's shop

*a puffer like the **Polar Light** which transported the team from Kames to a match at Inveraray on the occasion recounted opposite*

IN THE BEGINNING

Celly Paterson

The club was formed in 1896 (the year the first Camanachd Final was played) and was known as Kyles Athletic Football and Shinty Club, and in the first few years of its existence played football and shinty on alternate Saturdays.

The well-known Glasgow Cowal were instrumental in having the shinty seeds firmly sown on the 'Kerry shore' through one of their finest exponents, Sandy MacKellar, himself a Kylesman, and incidentally the first name engraved on the Glasgow Celtic Society Cup. Peter Ferguson, a native of Colintraive, helped in the coaching of the rudiments of caman play. Peter was the Millhouse blacksmith and it is said that if any player could strike the ball from the Smiddy door over the Powderwork dyke (about forty yards), he was in the team.

First president was Neil Nicolson, who with the able assistance of the headmasters D T Colquhoun and Arthur Barratt, George Irvine and Walter Brown, formed a committee which selected a team to travel and play the mighty Inveraray. Going from reports, this was quite an occasion. When the team left Kames Pier on the Puffer *Polar Light*, Piper MacFarlane playing them on their arduous journey up Loch Fyne. From all accounts he may have played a rousing march on entering the 'Ducal Town', but on the homeward trip it must have been a lament, because Kyles were trounced by eleven hails to nil, and to complete a disastrous outing, the *Polar Light* ran aground on Otter Spit.

Undismayed by this reverse the club, with apparently plenty of players, formed a league in the district, in which teams competed for a trophy donated by Donal Nicol of Ardmarnock, MP for Argyll.

The Powderworks at Millhouse gave much employment in the district, and on every New Year's Day a shinty match was arranged between two teams known as 'The Powder Monkeys' and 'The Sleeve Waistcoats' (local boys who worked on yachts during the season).

In 1900 Kyles took over the Moss as their home ground. (This field is home to the Ardlamont Sheepdog Trials and adjacent to the golf course, which opened in 1907.)

According to *The Buteman*, the Moss "had a surface like a billiard table, in tremendous order for a rousing game." (Readers will probably think G Y Slater was reporting even then). Kyles collected their first silverware in September 1900 when they won the handsome Buteman Challenge Cup at Rothesay. In the same year they changed their strip from narrow red and white horizontal stripes to their now familiar colours of Royal Blue, which were donated in the first instance by Rangers Football Club.

In 1901 they annexed the oldest trophy in the game, the Celtic Cup, under the captaincy of T R Nicolson. In 1904 the ultimate goal was achieved when they travelled to Kingussie and won the Camanachd Cup. The captain, Archibald Jamieson, was unable to play in the final as his hand was broken, so the vice-captain John MacKellar was the proud man who led Kyles to their first Camanachd victory.

That was to be the first of a hat-trick of victories for the Kylesmen, because in 1905 and 1906 the trophy returned to Tighnabruaich. I would like to point out, however, that those great victories were achieved with the able assistance of some great Lochfyneside names, players from Inveraray and Furnace who for some obscure reason had at some time or another thrown in their lot with the Royal Blue.

Among them were such great players as Ernest Smith, D Guthrie, D MacPhail, D Munro, T MacArthur, and A and M Sinclair. Some older readers may find it hard to believe that John S Ferguson (Pennymore) won three medals with Kyles.

When the Sir William Sutherland Cup for junior players was introduced in 1923, the area had junior teams in Tighnabruaich,

Kames, Millhouse, and Kilfinan, giving the Kyles committee an abundance of class juniors to choose from. In 1924 their youngsters brought the trophy home from Oban after defeating Newtonmore juniors 3-2.

Without records to refer to, I am truly indebted to my many friends – James Jamieson whose retentive memory was invaluable, Mrs Susan Symington for photographs, and James Middleton of *The Buteman* for research. I would also like to mention some of the surviving members of the old Kyles, now in the veteran category, who gave pleasure to innumerable people, the writer included – to players of Tighnabruaich, Kames, Millhouse, Kilfinan, and Col-Glen, rivals in junior competition who collectively formed Kyles Athletic and helped to make them great. They are 'Dudie' Weir, Donald Macrae, Willie MacKenzie, Donald Kent, John Kennedy. Robbie MacIntosh, John MacVicar, Archie Carmichael, and Archie Currie, all of whom were in a different playing generation to the writer.

This is an edited version of an article written by Celly Paterson. It appeared in *Kilfinan – Walks History Reminiscences* edited by H F Torbet and published by the Ardlamont Preservation Society in 1984.

THE KYLES

ALEXANDER MACKELLAR

Robert Murray, *The Celtic Monthly*, **Dec 1893**

Now that the ancient Highland game of shinty has again become popular, both in the straths of the north and towns in the south, it is interesting to refer to some of the prominent players of an older generation, who had done so much in their time to popularise our favourite pastime. Of these veterans few were better known ten or twelve years ago than Mr Alex Mackellar, the first captain of the Glasgow Cowal Shinty Club. Mr Mackellar is a native of Tighnabruaich, one of the most beautiful and favourite watering-places on the Cowal shore. In 1876 the subject of our sketch was the prime mover in forming the celebrated Glasgow Cowal Shinty Club, which, with the Edinburgh Camanachd, are the only clubs which have survived the vicissitudes of the intervening years. The Cowal men did wisely in electing Mr Mackellar to the post of captain, for he guided the fortunes of the club so well that for a period of eight years after their formation the Cowal team were undefeated. Perhaps this may be partly accounted for by the fact that Mr Mackellar induced his men to play the 'passing game', and anyone who has seen a match played on this scientific principle will understand the advantage which it gives the players who practise it. He has also substituted the leather ball for the old wooden one, which it will be admitted, was rather a dangerous article to play with.

Those were the palmy days of shinty in the south. The principal clubs at that time were the Edinburgh Camanachd, Vale of Leven, Ossian, Glasgow Camanachd, Glasgow Inveraray, Fingalians (later Glenforsa) and the Skye. Mr Mackellar captained his club in many stubborn contests during the eight years in which he held that office. Of these the most memorable, perhaps, were the match with the Glasgow Inveraray, on 26th April, 1879, for the Celtic Society's Challenge Cup, when Cowal defeated their opponents by 6 hails to 0; and in the following year the game with the Renton on their own ground, when the Cowal won by 3 hails to 1. Although Mr Mackellar no longer leads the Cowal men to the fray, he is the honorary president of the club, and feels proud that the Cowal team still hold their own on the shinty field, and are unversally acknowledged to be 'second to none' as exponents of the grand old game.

For ten years Mr Mackellar was a member of the Glasgow Highlanders (late 105th) during five of which he carried the colours, and before he retired he was offered a commission. It may be also mentioned that as an amateur all-round athlete he had few equals. The value of the silver plate trophies in his possession amounts to £100. He also possesses the championship medal for natives of Argyle for putting the stone.

Mr Mackellar was for many years director of the Cowal Society, and latterly acted as treasurer. He recently retired from business and is now residing at his Highland home in Cowal.

Notes:
It can fairly be said that modern shinty was invented in Glasgow and Edinburgh, and taught to the players in what are now its strongholds. Cowal certainly taught Kingussie a few lessons – too well, perhaps, since the pupils outdid the teachers in the first Camanachd final. Kyles played Cowal at the Rangers Highland Gathering, before a crowd of 10,000 at Ibrox. The game ended 1-1. Kyles had to use players from Inveraray and Cowal. Kyles' equaliser was scored by John MacKellar, of Cowal, a Kyles lad.

THE
GLASGOW CELTIC SOCIETY CUP

John MacLeod

On 31 October, 1856, a number of Highlanders in Glasgow met and decided to form a Society for the purpose of "Preserving and promoting the language, literature, music, poetry, antiquities and athletic games of the Highlanders". Other aims of the Society were the founding of bursaries to students of Highland descent and the encouragement of the wearing of Highland dress. Financial assistance was also afforded to city Highlanders in need.

A Constitution was drawn up and approved at the first AGM on February 5, 1857. As an example of the work done in those earlier years, it was stated at the annual dinner held in 1899 that, since the Society's inception,

> 1560 poor and deserving Highlanders had been relieved through its funds . . . sums totalling £337-4s. had been contributed in bursaries to Gaelic speaking students and in honoraria for the teaching of Gaelic . . . 100 guineas had been given towards the foundation of a Chair of Celtic at Edinburgh University . . . the sum of £211 had been spent on medals and prizes for Highland games, dancing and bagpipe playing. . . 275 distressed Highlanders had been provided with the means of returning from Glasgow to their homes, and of these 78 were sent to the Isle of Skye and 37 to the Oban district.

With the passage of the years, some of the original aims gradually became less relevant and although the present Society endorses those original aims when they are appropriate, it has for many years had as its primary aim the encouragement of the game of shinty. The trophy for the Glasgow Celtic Society Competition is the oldest in the sport, dating from 1879 when Glasgow Cowal, captained by A Mackellar, were the winners.

The first mention of Kyles Athletic in the minutes of the Glasgow Celtic Society is in 1899, when the club 'scratched' from an away tie against Oban in the competition for the Celtic Cup. No reason is given.

In the following year, Kyles Athletic reached the final and met Oban on 31 March, 1900. The match report in the *Glasgow Herald* of 2 April stated that "the Kyles team was at full strength, but the Oban lot (sic) were strengthened for the occasion by the inclusion of four players from the Ballachulish team." After 15 minutes, Kyles "opened out and transferred play to the other end of the field where Tom Nicolson, after dodging several opponents, scored with a clever right-hander."

This lead was held until twenty minutes into the second half when Oban equalised. "Great excitement now prevailed and it seemed as if the game would end in a draw, but, 5 minutes from the finish, McDougall again scored for Oban, who thus won a hard-fought battle by 2 goals to 1."

Kyles again reached the final the next year and, on 23 March 1901, under the captaincy of T Nicolson, recorded their first win by beating Glasgow Caledonian, in a competition in which Oban, Inveraray, Cowal, Perth and Edinburgh University had taken part. The attendance at the final at Moray Park Strathbungo, "was smaller than could have been wished for, but this was in a large degree owing to the early hour at which the match had to be started to enable the Kyles team to return home the same evening." (Glasgow Celtic Society minutes, 27 March 1901)

On 23 April 1903, Kyles, again captained by T Nicolson, had their second victory in the competition.

It may be of interest to note that the cost of badges to the winning team members was 3/- (15p) each and that as it was "impossible to provide refreshment for the teams at 1/- (5p) each . . . it was agreed that . . . 1/6 (7½p) per head be authorised . . . and not more than 40 to be entertained." (Glasgow Celtic Society minutes, 20 April 1904)

Kyles, led by D Fraser, next won the Cup in 1910, with a 4-0 victory over Strachur.

The competition was suspended in 1914, but when it was resumed, Kyles Athletic won four successive finals, from 1920-23, defeating Glasgow Skye in the last two of those triumphs, "by the odd goal in extra time of a replay after a 1-1 draw in 1922 . . . and by 4-1 in the 1922-23 season." (*Skye Camanachd – A Century Remembered* by Martin MacDonald)

The captains in those years were D Weir, M McGilp, J Nicolson, and W Greenshield. Again, it may be of interest to note that, in 1921, the directors of the Glasgow Celtic Society agreed to increase the donation to the clubs contesting the final from £1 to £1.10/- (£1.50).

In 1927, Kyles Athletic, led by D McRae, were successful once more and the team retained the Cup in each of the following two years under the captaincy of W McKenzie in 1928, and A Weir in 1929.

The 1930s were for Kyles a relatively lean period, with the Celtic Cup only coming twice to Tighnabruaich.

In 1933, the team skippered by R McIntosh was successful and, in 1939 there was another triumph when Glasgow Mid Argyll were beaten. The captain on this occasion was J Paterson.

(John Macleod's contribution derives from his research for the Centenary of the Society. A retired headteacher, he comes from Skye, and has played for Glasgow University, Kelvin and Glasgow Inverness-shire. Some local readers may remember him, as the Glasgow Inverness keeper who broke a goalpost at the Playing Field

Macrae Gilstrap of Ballimore – a generous supporter and one time 'Chieftain of Kyles Shinty Club'

1904 — THE BUILD-UP

**(The tone of this report suggests
it came from *The Buteman's* local reporter)**

The shinty final for the Scottish Cup should have been played in Glasgow. Fancy Kyles having to travel about a hundred miles, and Laggan, the other finalists, only having to travel eleven miles from their headquarters, and play on a field they are well accustomed to.

If the Kyles win, and we fancy they should if they go at it, as they can do when they care to spur themselves up a bit, it will be because they are easily the superior team, for the conditions are all against them.

The Kyles lads beg to thank their many friends in and of the Kyles district, in London, Glasgow, Rothesay, and elsewhere for their handsome donations, some of them sent unsolicited, to assist them in paying the expenses of their four days' journey to Kingussie to play off the final, and also for the good wishes which accompanied their welcome gifts.

Mr Nicolson had a very handsome donation sent from a most generous member and patron, the second within the last eight or ten weeks from the same quarter, and an accompanying note, a very nicely worded expression of the donor's good wishes. The secretary, too, received from a kind-hearted Rothesay gentleman, who takes a great interest in the game and has done much to advance its best interests, a handsome donation and "every success in the final". It is the like of this that puts life and vigour in the team and nerves their arms for the fray.

And Mr Walter Brown, the genial, jocular collector of the Kyles Club, has been on the warpath and got many scalps. We are informed he has been 'bleeding' the folks in the district financially with unwonted success even for him, securing over £6, and he still has a number of victims marked off for the 'treatment'.

The curious thing is that he uses his 'lancet' so skilfully that those who have undergone the operation weary till he comes round once more to perform it over again.

We were very pleased to see our old friend Mr John Bell, Furnace, at Otter Ferry. He is a keen follower of the game, and was of old one of the best players that ever handled a caman in Furnace. He was greatly taken with Tom Nicolson's display, and thinks that if Kyles had been without him Furnace would have won.

[The report begins with an account of a Kyles v Furnace game on a field at Otter Ferry "granted for the occasion by Major Macrae-Gilstrap of Ballimore, a generous patron and supporter and the Chieftain of the Kyles Shinty Club"]

The Kyles lads leave here on Friday morning, crossing to Kilmichael [Bute] and leave Glasgow (Buchanan Street Station) probably by the 2pm train, arriving in Kingussie about 7pm, where they will put up at Wolfenden's Hotel.

The match starts at 1.30. Lord Lovat is expected to present the cup to the winners. A big crowd is expected as great interest is being taken in the match.

There will be much excitement in Kames until the wire comes announcing the result, which we hope will be a happy one for Kyles. It will be a red-letter day in the history of the club if the Kyles lads crown all their previous achievements, and gain the title of Scottish champions.

They are in good trim, and will fight a gallant fight.

Their secretary got a beautiful picture postcard on Monday with these words on it – "Dear Mr Gemmell – Good luck to the Kyles. From an old admirer." All the way from New York.

Ballimore House, Otter Ferry today, home of early supporter Macrae Gilstrap and his son Duncan – in the early days many players would be employed on local estates

THE NICOLSONS

Sorley Maclean

My maternal grandfather was a Nicolson on both sides. He was a big, strong man who lived till he was ninety and was never known by himself or by any of his ten children to have been in bed even with half a day's illness until the last five days of his life. An East Coast skipper bringing meal to Braes mentioned "Big Sam handling bolls of meal as if they were pounds of tea."

He was a snob only in one way. I heard him only once referrring to his kinship to Nicolson of Sgoirebreac, the Chief of his name, and then he added that certain other families in Braes, Portree and Penefiles were nearer in blood to the Chief, but he frequently maintained that the 'big men of Kyles' were his relatives, descended from a brother of his grandfather, who married a farmer's daughter in South Argyll. My grandfather's grandfather was Somhairle MacIain MhicEoghainn, who was a piper in the Peninsular War and got wounded in the hands, and frostbite, in the retreat to Corunna in 1809. The Gaelic Eoghainn becomes Ewen in English in the North, but Hugh in Argyll; in the North the Gaelic Uisdean becomes Hugh.

In August 1920 the Portree Highland Games were renewed after the Great War. There was no Kyles Nicolson among the heavy athletes, but in 1921 John Nicolson, Broughty Ferry, was there with Starkey, Hector MacGregor etc, and among the light athletes were Donald and Ewen Kennedy (Donald was the grandfather of the Liberal MP). John Nicolson was said to have worsted the legendary A A Cameron in wrestling when he (Nicolson) was only eighteen. At the end of the Games John Nicolson 'coached' the Braes tug-o-war team, who won.

Among the Braes eight there must have been four Nicolsons. I forget who they all were but the 'anchor' was Alasdair Nicolson, uncle of the noted Skye and Glasgow Skye shinty players, Sammy, Johnny and Nicol Bain. Of course there were at that time other powerful men in Braes who were not Nicolsons by name.

Sorley Maclean was headteacher of Plockton High School until his retiral some twenty years ago. He has had a lifelong interest in schools shinty and in Skye Camanachd. But he is best known as a poet in the great tradition of the Gaelic Bards – widely recognised to be the greatest in this century.

Four of the legendary Nicolson brothers on their way to a Camanachd final by train – (l to r) Andrew, Jock, Calum and Jimmy

BROTHERS

Andrew Nicolson

Neil Nicolson was born in 1849. He was brought up in Campbeltown and left there to take up farming in the Kyles of Bute. The father of the Nicolsons under review stood 6'3" tall and was expert enough in athletics to annex local championships in his youth. He was also one of the 'fathers' of Kyles Athletic.

Of ten sons, the second youngest (Celestine) died as the result of war wounds. Eight achieved outstanding fame in athletics and sports generally, whilst several were enrolled as authentic champions each in his particular sport.

Neil, the oldest son, farmed at Auchgoyle. He repeatedly won the Duke of Argyle Trophy for the County Championships in all round athletics. He was a natural athlete – successful in the hammer, hop step and leap, shot putt, high jump, sprint, and Cumberland wrestling. After retiring from active athletics he took up shooting and golf and became an expert at both, holding the course record of the Kyles of Bute Golf Course for many years.

Hugh farmed at Achdalvorie. He was one of the foremost games athletes touring Scotland, excelling in the shot, hammer, wrestling and caber. He played full centre for Kyles.

Tom farmed at Corra. He was Captain of Kyles, a world-class hammer thrower (see below), and also excelled at golf and football – he became friendly with Celtic Manager Willie Maley, and they used to travel together to all the sports meetings.

In the days before taxicabs were plying for hire in the streets of London, Tom Nicolson and some brother Scots on a southern pilgrimage in search of championship laurels had occasion to travel by hansom cab.

The Cockney Jehu, noticing Tom's handbag, volunteered to take the valise on the top luggage rack, and leant over to receive the bag. Although it contained hammer throwing missiles in duplicate, TR tossed it up as any ordinary person might throw a hat box. The unsuspecting cabman on taking delivery was catapulted backwards. However, TR knew what was likely to happen and was ready to catch baggage and cabman before they hit the pavement.

Harry Lauder was a regular visitor at Corra. He and TR had a wonderful rapport. Harry left his pet pony 'Beauty' and TR used the pony with trap for his early milk round. 'Beauty' disappeared during the war when vast areas of the Kyles were taken over by the army.

George farmed at Kildavaig, James at Auchgoyle, and Malcolm at Fearnoch. These three were the backbone of the Kyles team which regularly won Championship honours. They were not as well known in athletic circles as their older brothers, but all three were capable of class performances over the whole heavy event spectrum. Malcolm, particularly, could best any visiting professional in the shot or wrestle. He was also a Physical Training Instructor in the army.

Jock, who joined the Partick Police and later became a Shore Porter in Dundee, was the giant of the lot. The brothers averaged 6' and 15st but Jock exceeded the that by 2" and 2st. He competed in all the tournaments over a period of 17 years, winning frequently with the 16lb and 20lb hammer. He was also a great weight thrower, and probably his best was 70' with the 28lb weight at Barr's Sports at Celtic Park – probably a world record at the time. He won the Cumberland wrestling as and when he wanted. I often wonder how any opponent managed to clasp their hands round that frame.

He was reckoned in his day to be the strongest man in all Britain. It was John Strong of England who bore that out. Strong, Champion Cumberland wrestler, challenged the world with the remark that the man who could raise his 20st off the ground would be the first to be beat him. Jock took up the challenge at the Glasgow Police Sports at Celtic Park when he was a stripling of twenty one. He flipped Strong twice off his ponderous legs and twice laid him on his back.

Jock played shinty for Kyles, but was the only brother not to win a Championship medal.

Celestine had shown signs of following the family athletics tradition before the First World War. He, too, represented Kyles at shinty. Dougie died aged 12.

Andrew, the youngest, was a member of the Glasgow Police. He and TR were the only members of the family to remain amateur. He was also good at discus, hop step and jump, long jump, and golf. There are many who believe that if he had seriously devoted himself to the shot he would have reached the top in the world.

He played for Kyles for many years at full centre. It is interesting to note that six of the brothers played for Kyles at the same time, and that the other three preceded them.

One year in Oban when four of the family lined up in the Kyles cup-winning team, the then Lord Lovat who was to present the trophy asked Nicolson senior, "Just how many of a family have you got?"

"Sir," said 6'3" farmer Nicolson, "I've been blessed with ten sons – and every one of them has a sister." That, if you will see if you are as quick on the uptake as was the noble lord, makes only one sister.

What brothers were hers.

Note:
The sister was Mary. Her descendants include the Patersons, well represented in this book – and David Taylor, captain of Kyles cup-winning 1994 team.

T R Nicolson and Andrew Nicolson

(from an article in *Athletics Weekly*, 6/2/82, by John W Keddie)

Born in 1878, Hugh Nicolson first travelled to the Scottish AAA Championships in 1899, held at Hampden Park, where he finished second in the shot putt, as he did on his next visit in 1901. But in 1902 Hugh easily won the title and the following month he won the shot in the Scotland v Ireland international in Dublin. But, alas, it was the last to be seen of him in the amateur arena. The lure of the professional games was too great. The measure of the loss to the amateur scene may be gauged by the fact that in 1904 at the Cowal Gathering he set a shot record of 14.40, a distance no Scottish amateur bettered for nigh on fifty years!

Younger brother Thomas Rae (born in 1879) was certainly a good all-rounder. Not only did he have an aptitude for the throwing events, but he was a great shinty player, a promising footballer and a good wrestler. But his domain was the shot and hammer, especially the latter, at which he was to become truly outstanding – one of the few who could challenge the predominance of the Irish-American throwers of the day.

Tom's first appearance in the Scottish Amateur Athletics Association Championships was in 1901, when he placed third in the shot and second in the hammer with frankly modest performances. At the Scoto-Irish match in Glasgow, he saw great hammer throwing for probably the first time when the famed Irish all-rounder Tom Kiely launched the 16lb wire-handled hammer 44.30m – 10.02m further than his own best throw. This contest marked Tom's first efforts with a wire-handled hammer. His subsequent improvement was dramatic. Through diligent practice on his farm at Millhouse he went from strength to strength. From that day when as a 23-year-old he won his first Scottish hammer title he achieved an amazing nineteen consecutive wins up to 1924, won again in 1926 and 1927, and even came back in 1929, aged fifty, to take second place.

We have said that Tom's record-breaking exploits began in 1902. Well, the following year he seemed to break his native record almost every time out. In May, June, July and August he improved the record by stages to 46.44. And he set a new native record to win the first of fourteen SAAA shot titles.

51

This was the culmination of a great year which saw him win the shot and hammer at the AAA Championships at the Northampton Cricket Ground.

That was the only time that Tom won the AAA shot, though he was second four times and third once. In the hammer he was as invincible as he was on the Scottish scene, winning on every appearance until 1914. Meanwhile, in the Scoto-Irish internationals he had a wonderful series of successes between 1903 and 1913, winning on all but two occasions. His best winning effort in the series was 50.32 in 1912.

But to go back in time for a moment, we have already mentioned Tom's record-breaking feats of 1903. The following season he was to prove himself one of the best throwers in the world at that time. At the Rangers Sports he threw an 'American-style' 16lb hammer 51.72m from a 9' circle, and the following week at Celtic Sports he reached 50.54. But that year the standard circle size had been established at seven feet, and neither was recognised as a native record. In due course he did improve his native record under acceptable conditions, reaching 49.58 in the 1908 Championships, followed later that season by 50.20 at the Rangers Sports and finally 50.84 at a Scotland v America contest at Saughton Park, Edinburgh. As a native record Tom's distance was unsur–passed for thirty-nine years, and as a British best for fifteen.

Tom Nicolson made two appearances in the Olympic Games, first in 1908 when in London he placed fourth with 48.09, then in 1920 in Antwerp where he placed sixth in unusual circumstances. Commitments on the farm prevented him getting to the stadium in time for the preliminaries. But so well-known and popular was Tom among officials and competitors alike that qualification for the final was waived in his case.

And Tom did well enough in the circumstances, placing sixth with 45.70. Just ahead of Tom was Matt McGrath who is reported as having said that if Tom had gone to the States he would surely have won an Olympic title. But Tom had a farm to run, and that was more important.

It may be appropriate here to summarise Tom's SAAA Championship record over the twenty-eight years he competed: shot 14 wins, 4 seconds; wire hammer 21 wins, 2 seconds; Scots hammer 3 wins; 56 lb weight 4 wins, 1 second. Forty-two Championship wins! Surely a record which marks him out as the most successful competitor in Scottish Championship history. For durability and consistency the career of Tom Nicolson is without peer.

As William Reid put it in the SAAA Jubilee volume (1933): We may have another Liddell, but it is not likely that we shall ever have another Tom Nicolson, most modest of great athletes, most lovable of sportsmen. He will ever rank as the greatest heavy athlete Scottish amateur athletics has ever boasted. His best individual achievement may be beaten but there surely never will be a career so long and full of honours as that of the genial Kyles farmer.

Andrew Coats Nicolson was one of the youngest of the family. He was nineteen years Tom's junior and served with the Glasgow Police all his working life. It was in 1924 that he succeeded Tom as SAAA shot champion, and between that date and 1936, with the exception of 1929 when he was absent and 1932 when he was placed second, Andrew won the title. As late as 1939 – twenty years after his first appearance – Andrew placed third in the shot.

He gained 41 SAAA medals in all (including 11 victories in the shot and 5 in the Scots hammer), bringing the Nicolson family total to 95 (59 of them first places)! Thus from 1899, when Hugh first placed in in SAAA shot, up 1939 the Nicolsons almost totally dominated the event in Scotland, with 26 successes out of a possible 37.

Hugh died in 1967, aged 87. This was two years after Andrew. Tom had passed away in 1971, aged 71. He was buried in the cemetry of the Church of Scotland in Kilbride. No obituary notices appeared in the national press. But the most remarkable character in Scottish athletic history had passed from the scene.

A full account of the careers of T R and Andrew can be found in the same author's *Scottish Athletics 1883-1983* – the SAAA's centenary history.

THE DISTRICT

FROM THE WATER

Summer Tours
in
Scotland
Glasgow to the Highlands
The
Royal Route
by
David MacBrayne's
Royal Mail Steamers
"Columba," "Iona" &c.

Official Guide – New Edition
(Reprinted from the 1895 orginal
by Famedram Publishers)

The steamer next touches at Colintraive, the nearest landing place for Glendaruel. At this pier some groups of passengers usually land, on pleasant picnicing intent, as there are many delightful walks in the neighbourhood. Leaving Colintraive we sail through the Kyles or narrows of Bute proper, and here the scenery increases in interest and beauty. The strip of water is very contracted, there being only a little more than sufficient width to allow our steamer to pass through between the mainland on our right and the Island of Bute on our left.

The tourist who for the first time sails through this strait is at a loss to know how the steamer can possibly proceed further, as the high steep hills in front seem to shut it entirely in, until he begins to notice an arm, as it were, of the sea to his right and another to his left; but which one is likely to be taken is puzzling. The one to the right (Loch Ridden) extends six miles inland to Ormidale and Glendaruel. As the steamer turns to the left, Loch Ridden opens up in all its grandeur, and is indeed a sight well worth remembering. Here we have glen and mountain, loch and stream, with, if it be calm, the reflection of the hills in the bright green water, so that at every turn new and more exciting beauties are disclosed.

At the entrance to Loch Ridden is a little low island (Eilean Dheirg) marked by a solitary tree. This was the scene of the failure of the Earl of Argyll's expedition in 1685, so graphically described by Macaulay. The castle we now pass is Glen Caladh, recently the property of George Robert Stephenson, of Newcastle, nephew of the great engineer. Almost directly opposite, on the Bute shore, are the "Maids of Bute", two rocks on a green spot upon the hill, resembling two maidens sitting side by side. A few minutes more and, after turning to our right at Rhubaan Point, we call at the pretty village of Tighnabruaich, an enjoyable seaside retreat.

Tighnabruaich is a Gaelic word, denoting "House of the Brae", as there was for a long time but one house there; of late, however, the place has increased very much. We next pass Kames, where there are large Powder Mills, but everything of an explosive nature is manufactured more than two miles from the shore on the road which strikes across to Loch Fyne. Looking before us we see the low-lying island of Inchmarnock, and further off the Holy Isle. Rounding Ardlamont Point a good view is to be had of Ardlamont House, situated to our right amongst beautiful trees. This mansion house was the seat of the Chief of the Clan Lamont. In the distance away to the south, the island of Arran can be seen to advantage, with its loftiest mountain "Goatfell" towering 3000 feet above the sea.

THE KYLES

THE DISTRICT
— SOME EARLY HISTORY

Rev Ean M Simpson

The first residents of the Kyles were hunters of the late stone age (c 2000BC) living in rude shelters of skins and branches. Recent excavations at Macewen's Castle has brought to light worked flint scrapers of the period. Wild boar roamed the countryside at Kames and provided food, clothing and fuel for the nomads.

Permanent reminders of these earliest inhabitants abound, ranging from the chambered cairn at Carn Ban through Bronze Age standing stones (eg at Kames Cross Roads), at Tighnabruaich, Achnaha, Kilfinan and Stillaig, through the Ardmarnoch Cist to the Iron Age vitrified forts and duns to be found on many of the hilltops.

The Parish of Kilfinan takes it name from the cell of Finan, a monk, who came to the district from Iona in 565. The oldest building in the Parish was the church, dedicated to Finan in about 651. Although the present structure dates mostly from 1759, it stands in an ancient graveyard in which are to be found stones dating from medieval Christian times, some of which have been made easily accessible in the seventeenth century Lamont Vault against the North Wall of the Kirk.

The Vikings raided the Parish area, particularly at Otter on Loch Fyne. (Otter does not take its name from that beautiful animal, but from the Norse *oitir*, meaning a spit of land). On one raid, in 918, Danish longships landed on Otter Spit and the Danes received a terrible hammering from the local inhabitants. The defeated sea-raiders were driven away from their fleet and across the Bealloch to Glendaruel, where they received yet another mauling from the locals there. The dead were thrown into the river which became known as the Ruel from that day, ruel being a corruption of the Gaelic word for red (referring to the bloody stain in the water).

In the thirteenth century, King Alexander II visited the area and subjugated it. His daughter, Princess Christiana, married Malmory (brother of the then Lamont chief) and lived at Achdalvorie – known then as Achety Malmory – the field of Malmory.

The Lamonts were the chief family in the Parish and for long centuries the chiefs of the clan lived at Ardlamont House. Ascog Castle was a Lamont stronghold until the Campbells burned it after a battle in 1644. The ruin still stands.

To the north of the Lamont lands lay Ardgaddan, where dwelt the Macewens who gave their name to the 'castle' whose foundations are still visible near Kilfinan. The Macewens were a friendly clan who intermarried with the Lamonts and Maclachlans on either side of them. They, too, were ousted by the Campbells in 1450.

Kilfinan Hotel was an old coaching inn at one time, and it has a splendid cellar dating from 1500, still to be seen.

When Charles I lost his cause and was on the way to losing his head also, the pro-Royalist Sir James Lamont immediately fortified Ascog Castle against expected Campbell plundering.

On June 1st, 1644, the long-awaited attack came and following a big battle on the moors above the castle, the Lamonts surrendered – on condition that they should be allowed their lives. But the Campbells broke their word and the Lamonts not slaughtered on the spot were taken to Dunoon and hanged.

The following year, the Lamonts and some Irish irregulars mustered at Kilfinan seeking revenge on the Covenanting Campbells. Along with the whole Covenanting Presbytery of Dunoon, the Kilfinan minister fled to the safety of the Lowlands until the rising had been put down.

In 1656, the Argyll ministers met twice in Kilfinan Kirk to finalise the Gaelic translation of the Psalter. The Kilfinan minister himself was responsible for the translation of the Book of Ruth.

In 1721, the Millhouse Smith was charged by the Kirk Session with using the Black Arts. It seemed that the Smith, a man who dearly loved a drink and a fight, was deemed to have effected cures of sick children "by a charm, pretending to heal them through the powers of so many Smiths, his forefathers, by laying the children upon the anvil there several days of the week, drawing the hammer in a threatening manner against the child's body and repeating some words." To be effective, however, there had to be money under the child's body!

Achnaskeoch lies roughly midway between Kilfinan and Tighnabruaich. In 1745, James Stewart JP of Achnaskeoch, an elder in Kilfinan Kirk and a highly respected landowner, was to accompany his brother-in-law, the Chief of Clan Maclachlan, with an armed force to Edinburgh where they hoped to join Bonnie Prince Charlie. Was it feminine intuition which moved his wife to decide that James would *not* go? The night before he was due to travel, Mrs Stewart 'accidentally' spilt boiling water over his legs, thus incapacitating him safely for the time being, for which James Stewart probably had cause to be grateful. For in the butchery following Culloden the Maclachlan lost most of his estate and his family home, while James Stewart of Achnaskeoch continued to flourish. The old house is no more, but many of the stones went to the building of Drum Bridge.

During the French Wars of the early nineteenth century, according to local legend, a widow's son from Millhouse was dragged at the tail of a cart by the Navy Pressgang to Ardlamont. He died as a result of his injuries – and the widow prophesied that the Lamonts would lose their land bit by bit until only Ardlamont was left. Coincidentally or not, the prophecy came true!

Smuggling was rife at the Kerry end of the Parish (Tighnabruaich, Kames and Ardlamont) and the inhabitants carried on a roaring trade in French Brandy from the Isle of Man. The story is told of a group of grateful smugglers who presented a 'gallery' to Kilfinan Kirk – which became known to every soul in the district (except the minister!) as 'The Brandy Lads Gallery'.

(From *The Kyles of Bute, Argyll* – published by The Kyles of Bute Improvements Trust)

An early picture of Tighnabruaich Curling Club

TIGHNABRUAICH CURLING CLUB

Archie MacLeod

At a meeting held in Tighnabruaich Hotel on 17th December, 1878, the undernoted persons agreed a resolution to form a Curling Club, to be called the Tighnabruaich and Millhouse Curling Club: Messrs D Gunn, R Duncan, J Duncan Jnr, J Scott, J McCallum, J Dalton, T Dobie, and L Davies. Mr D Gunn was elected President and Mr R Duncan, Honorary Secretary. It was proposed and agreed that the Entrance Fee and Annual Subscription be 2/6 (12½p) per member.

At the present day, 118 years on, the club has a playing strength of some twenty six active members, and under the Presidency of Ronnie Brown competes for all Argyll Province and local trophies and has representative rinks in two evening leagues at Drimsynie Leisure Centre. A notable advance from 1878 is the Annual Membership fee which now stands at £10 per member! It's a terrible thing the inflation.

It would require a lengthy tome and an able pen to record the progress and successes of the club together with the many well-known Kyles names who have been associated with it in the intervening years since 1878 but some of the highlights are perhaps worthy of mention.

In true democratic fashion the annual general meetings rotated through Tighnabruaich, The Royal and Kames hotels, the first being referred to in some minutes as The Blair Arms. This rather high-sounding name may awaken memories in the oldest of Kyles residents since it was synonymous with its more commonly used soubriquet, The Gluepot.

Around 1880 there appears to have been in existence a Kilfinan Curling Club. The 1882 minutes record the Tighnabruaich Club secretary being instructed to write to Kilfinan Club proposing an amalgamation.

No reply appears to have been forthcoming from Kilfinan, and thereafter the Tighnabruaich secretary each year when mentioning prizes and competitions states rather pointedly "open to Tighnabruaich Club Members (only)".

A major event in the early years was the acceptance of Tighnabruaich Curling Club into Membership of the Royal Caledonian Curling Club, which is recorded in 1895. The prime mover in this matter appears to have been a Mr W Watson who is recorded as a member of both the Tighnabruaich Club and the Royal Caledonian. The Initiation of the Club and its members took place in the Royal Hotel on 10th March, 1896, when three members of the Rothesay Curling Club attended the Initiation Ceremony. Provost Milloy of Rothesay occupied the position of My Lord of the Court with Mr Buchanan of the Rothesay Club as his Officer assisted by Mr MacKirdy of the Rothesay Club and Mr Watson of the Tighnabruaich Club and RCCC.

The Tighnabruaich secretary records that the Rothesay members "went to the business with great spirit" but no doubt conducted with the dignity and decorum normally associated with this event. Thereafter in those early years the club held a Court at regular intervals wherein new members were duly initiated.

There have been many stalwart supporters over the years but it is of interest that in 1895 the secretary was instructed to inform by letter D M Nicol Esq MP and Mrs D N Nicol also S Millar Esq and Mrs S Millar that they had been "nominated as first patrons and patronesses of the Tighnabruaich Curling Club".

The club has curled at various venues prior to 1899 when a proposal was put forward to build a Club Pond on Hafton Farm, Auchenlochan Estate, the proprietor Laird being Malcolm of Poltalloch. In due course a lease was concluded with the proprietors for the rent of one acre at the nominal fee of 1/- per annum. In due course an estimate of £60 was accepted from a Mr John O'Donnell, the pond was duly completed and in 1901 a competition on the new pond was arranged with the Rothesay Club.

The secretary records triumphantly in 1901, "we have a pond equal to none in Scotland". One of the financial depressions which most clubs experience from time to time appears to have hit the club that same year, when it was agreed that there would be no Annual Dinner "as the funds is low in the secretary's hands at the moment".

Although there were some years of mild winters which allowed of little activity, the 'new pond' provided many happy days' curling, though in later years Meldalloch was an equally popular venue following an agreement with Colonel Nicol of Ardmarnoch for the use of the loch.

These few historical notes reflect the formation of a local club which has existed for nearly 120 years and which at present is as numerically strong and enthusiastically supported as at any time in its history.

It must be mentioned however that the curlers of today have an advantage which our forfathers never knew, and that is the facility of 'inside ice'.

The Province Championship, the Chalmers Quaich, the Nicol Cup, the MacQuistan Cup, the Tappit Hen, and the Inveraray Shield are among the many trophies which are keenly entered by the clubs which form the Argyll Province, these in addition to local competitions between clubs in different districts of the Province.

The certainty of playing all competitions regardless of weather, the regular camaraderie in meeting members of clubs both in and without the Argyll Province is a bonus which I am sure the 'old brigade' of the last century and the first half of this would have relished to the full.

THE KYLES

CAMANS CROSS THE WATER

Douglas MacFie

The first organised Shinty Club was formed on the Island of Bute in 1907 but the game had been played across the island in a 'bounce match' from as far back as the then living memory.

The feats of Kyles Athletic in winning the Camanachd Cup in 1904, 1905, and 1906 all on Northern soil stirred up intense interest on the island. They also led to Captain Colin MacRae of Ballimore wishing to increase the number of clubs entering the Ballimore Cup donated by his brother Major MacRae Gilstrap. He met with Lord Bute and a meeting was held on the island in 1907 at which Bute Camanachd was formed. Their home pitch was the Meadows. A few weeks later North Bute Shinty Club was formed. Their home pitch was at Ettrick Bay.

Alex Mackellar of Rhubaan, a recognised Shinty 'guru' of the time, assisted the Bute teams with their practice matches, bringing over as many as ten 'expert' Kyles players for these matches. Alex Mackellar himself turned out for Bute in goal in some of Bute Camanachd's early games.

Mackellar's Rhubaan Royal Rovers team were regular visitor to the island, particularly for the New Year's Day Gala matches which also featured Tug o' War contests. In 1909 the Rhubaan team was: Alex Mackellar, Donald Fraser, Donald MacLachlan, John McArthur, Archie McCallum, John Thomson, Robert Thomson, Daniel McArthur, John McKellar, Donald McCallum, John Warden, and Peter McVicar.

Captain, later Major, Colin MacRae was himself a driving force in the spread of Shinty in the area, bringing over his Ballimore team which played in a colourful red and green strip contrasting with the Bute Camanachd's white strip. He was a fine player himself and was a regular goal scorer. He later played for Col-Glen. The Kyles and Ballimore teams often travelled to the island on steamships such as the *Tingal* and the *Benmore*.

The Bute teams could not hope to match the then Kyles team in the senior trophies but set their sights on the junior trophies such as the Ballimore, Buteman and McPherson cups. They soon reached their first final in 1909, the Buteman Cup against Kames. Disaster struck. The Meadows was double booked with a territorial parade taking preference. Despite being informed of this, Kames turned up and claimed the cup by default. Captain MacRae arbitrated in Kames favour.

Bute went on to distinguish themselves at junior level, contesting the first ever Sutherland Cup final, going down to Newtonmore 3-2 at Roy Bridge in 1923. The club's proudest moment was in 1972 when they won the Sutherland Cup, beating what was to become a great Aberdeen University team in the final. In 1985 the club was also the first winner of the resurrected Ballimore Cup as a national trophy, beating Glengarry 3-2 at Spean Bridge.

They still strive to reach the highest standards of shinty achieved by their neighbours and friends across the Kyles of Bute. The nearest achieved to date was in 1980 when Bute led the South Division I for most of the season, having defeated Kyles Athletic 4-1 at the Meadows. They almost completed the dosage in the Camanachd Cup, leading Kyles well into the second half. Kyles went on to win a memorable final 6-5 against Newtonmore. Near things do not go into record books however, so Bute must learn what makes teams like Kyles winners!

Over the years the links between Kyles and Bute have always been strong. Many players from the Kyles area have graced the Bute colours and more than a few Butemen have worn the famous blue of Kyles. Which reminds me of the occasion of a Camanachd Cup final when Newtonmore had just scored their sixth of seven goals.

Celly Paterson turned to his substitute (a Bute great of the past).

"On you go and see what you can do." The player's reply is unprintable, frustrated as he was at not getting on earlier when he might have had a chance of making a difference. Ah, well, maybe there are occasions when it is just as well there is a strip of water between us!

Junior shinty thrived pre-World War II – (above) Tighnabruaich 1926 and (below) Millhouse 1921

RECOLLECTIONS

John Paterson

My uncles were all sportsmen and from a very early age I tried to emulate them in some of their games and of course shinty was one of them. I would be about seven years old when I first spectated at a big match – Kyles against Glasgow Cowal on the Magazine field when Kyles won 1-0. I never saw my uncles Neil, Hugh or Tom play for the Kyles although I learned a lot about shinty by just talking to them. I remember Uncle Tom telling me that he thought Ernest Smith of Inveraray was the best player he had ever seen.

I was born in 1914 and was the first baby that the Rev CVA MacEachern, newly appointed minister to the Kilfinan Parish, ever christened. I was held by my granny Nicolson at Auchgoyle. I can remember her very clearly, but cannot recall much about my grandfather Niall Mhor, the man who had so much to do with the Kyles.

I played for the Millhouse school team when I was about nine in the Ainsworth Medal, and I can remember that Dougie Campbell of Ascog was Captain and full back. Malcolm John Currie, Bogie Ferguson, Ian MacNeill and my brother Neil were all in the team too and we were thrashed 6-0 by Tighnabruaich. There seemed to be an awful lot of Curries in the Tighnabruaich team.

At that time there were only cup games being played and great events they were. Of course very few people saw the away games through lack of transport and the result was always sent by telegram. When Kyles had a victory, Big Peter MacCallum of the Post Office at Millhouse would come out to the door of the shop and wave his

69

white apron. My granny or mother would be watching at the parlour window in Auchgoyle just to get the result. There was always great sadness when the apron didn't wave – defeat.

During my schooldays I loved shinty more than anything else and had all my heroes in the Kyles. Looking back a lot of fine characters spring to mind.

Dudie Weir and Willie Greenshields (blacksmith), great forwards; uncles Calum and Andrew Nicolson in the centre line; Allan MacFadyen and Neil (Stiff) MacGilp who were supreme at half-back; and what a pair uncles George and Jimmy were at full back. Then of course the last line of defence – Dolly MacFadyen, unbeatable in goal. At that time Kyles also used players from Lochgoilhead and Ardentinny and the ones I remember are Willie Armstrong, Donald and Calum Fraser, and Willie MacKenzie.

Shinty up to the thirties was played without penalties being awarded for fouls – a good job too. I can remember seeing Jimmy Nicolson throwing his arms round Tommy MacArthur's neck and bringing him to the ground thus saving a certain goal. That was in a game Kyles v Furnace at the Moss.

Inveraray and Kyles were always great rivals and both teams produced many gifted players. The head-to-head clashes I will always remember were those between Andrew Nicolson of Kyles and D Campbell (Deecam). One or the other or both were regularly sent off for fighting. In later years the main battle was always between Duncan Currie (Bunks) and Neil MacGugan with Bunks nearly always coming out on top.

I played for Millhouse Juniors before being promoted to the big team and can remember some great tussles with Archie (Seedy) Marshall of Kames and Ian Irvine of Tighnabruaich. What a pity Ian couldn't use his glasses – he was terribly shortsighted. I won a Scottish Junior medal playing for Kyles Juniors at Mossfield, Oban, against Newtonmore and from there became a fully-fledged senior player.

We won the Scottish Cup in 1935 and I think the team of that year was about the best Kyles had ever put on the field. The game was played at the Bught Park, Inverness, against Caberfeidh and it was at that game I learned a wee bit about some folk's superstitions.

70

We had to pass a cemetry on the road to the hotel and we had to be played on to the field to the tune of the *Glendaruel Highlanders*. My last match for the Kyles was in the Celtic Cup final in Glasgow in 1939 when I was captain. We won and I am the proud owner of a silver-mounted stick. That year we lost in the final of the Scottish and I got a second caman made by Ronald McColl.

When we played at Inveraray we always sailed across from St Catherine's by motor boat and I can remember all the team laughing at uncle Hugh Nicolson with a hand on each gunwale trying to keep the boat in the drills.

When we played at Inverness in 1935, both George Symington and I had had all our teeth extracted and were awaiting new dentures. I can remember my opponent of the day, big Tom Cameron, who was 6'6" tall and weighed sixteen stone, telling me that it was the first time he had been well beaten by a toothless whitrack (weasel). I took his remark as a compliment.

Playing against Oban Camanachd on the Winterton at Inveraray, I was knocked out for a few minutes by my opponent's stick across my face, and when I came to, all I could see was uncle Jimmy holding him off the ground by the neck.

He told the crowd he would lay him (Brown) down as soon as I got up – then told me not to come home unless I nailed my opponent before the end of the game. I did. After the match the referee, Duncan MacPhedran, said to me that he had never seen me commit a deliberate foul, and fortumnately for me his eyes were shut when I broke my stick across Brown's knee.

John Paterson is a brother of the late Celly, uncle of the current Kyles President of the same name, and grand-uncle of David Taylor, the 1994 winning captain.

71

Henry MacKendrick

My earliest recollections of Kames is starting school holidays when I was about five years old. We travelled by train from Glasgow Central to Greenock Princes Pier or Gourock and from there got 'the boat'. The boat! Oh, the boats!

The first glimpse of the boats was the start of our holidays. There were the yellow funnelled boats of the Caledonian Steam Packet Co, run in conjunction with the LMS Railway Co. They owned the *Jupiter, Glen Sannox, Duchess of Argyll* and many others. The red funnels of the *Iona* and *Columba*, the mail boats, and others owned by MacBrayne's. These two companies are now Calmac. Then there were the red, white and black funnels of the LNER Railway Co boats like the *Jeanie Deans*, which sailed from Helensburgh. Or if you wanted to sail all the way from Glasgow you could take Williamson Buchanan's white-funnelled *Eagle, Kylemore, King Edward, Queen Mary* and others from the Broomielaw.

There were many boats we knew by sight as soon as they came into view. From Gourock the boats would call at Kirn, Dunoon, Innellan, Craigmore, Rothesay, Port Bannatyne, sometimes Colintraive, and less frequently Ormidale, and then it was through the Kyles to Tighnabruaich. There you started to pick up the bags, baskets, suitcases and hampers tied with ropes, then fight you way in the queue to the gangway, ready to disembark at Auchenlochan and look out for MacBride's, Turner's or Simpson's taxi to take you up the Smiddy Brae and drop you off outside Berryburn. Old Berryburn, you wouldn't recognise it now.

At that time there was MacBride's garage and workshops, two old-fashioned petrol pumps, and the fuel lifeline of the community – paraffin oil. Every household needed it for cooking, heating and lighting. Above that was Berryburn – Wee Berryburn, and Big Berryburn, our destination. Climb up the wooden stairs to the top and carry all the luggage including the hampers which had to be left and emptied on the top landing outside , and that was you there. You had arrived at last!

The flat at Berryburn, with its outside downstairs WC, was first rented by my grandmother MacKendrick, then by my mother, and when she died my father's sister Aunt Maggie Munro took over the lease.

Grandmother had a family of four sons and six daughters, so when it came to summer holidays they had to rent other accommodation at Kyles View, Kyles Cottage, Albion House and others. Often there were more than forty of us here at one time. We had two picnics each week – one afternoon to Ostel Bay and a full day to Otter Ferry. MacBride's bus would make two journeys, sometimes three, plus the cars. The children would gather timbers and rub together two flint stones to the light the fire. The mothers then cooked the meals.

That's where most of the families coming from Glasgow learned to swim – at the Kyles. To many of us there is no place like it in the world.

I can remember many days when after running barefoot down roads to the shore the first thing that greeted you on your return home was mother, standing at the door with a large lump of butter which she placed in your hand to rub the tar off your feet before you were allowed to enter the house.

By the time I had reached eleven or twelve years of age I did the baker's round with Dougie MacCallum. His brother Ronnie did the other round. I would go down to 'Cameron's Corner' where we would listen to the 'old men' (none of them as old as I am now) who sat on a bench beside the old weighing machine and told yarns more interesting than any of the books I would take to read and while away the time.

When visitors arrived we were allowed to take out an old flat-bottomed punt and bring in two rowing boats which we had to bail out for them. The only reward I ever received was when it came to about ten minutes to six and the proprietor would say, "Right, young

73

MacKendrick, you can take the punt out for ten minutes but see that you get back here before six o' clock. Some of the visitors will be waiting for a boat." Such generosity sometimes amazed me!

Mind you, most of the customers would give me a penny, sometimes even two, and quite often a rich customer would surreptitiously place a whole silver threepenny piece in my hand for helping them in and out of the boat. But mostly it was the thrill and privilege of being allowed to work the boats that pleased me most. These were great days.

Then of course there was the golf club. My cousin and I were introduced by John Symington, whose father was the local chemist and Neil Dewar, whose parents owned the fruit and vegetable shop in Tighnabruaich. For a fee of half-a-crown we had a locker and junior membership. However at the following AGM it emerged there was to be no junior membership, so we had our fees returned, but were immediately reinstated as full members. We were then about twelve years of age.

On a Saturday morning after finishing the baker's round I would rush into the house, pick up a sandwich and dash out without even sitting down. Mother would call, "What's all the rush? Where are you running to now?"

"They're playing shinty at Rhubaan today," I would say.

Kyles Athletic have always commanded the greatest respect from all the leading teams throughout Scotland. For me their greatest achievement was winning the Glenmorangie Cup in the final against Fort William at the Bught Park Inverness on the 4th of June 1994 – a day and a date I shall never forget. Fort William were odds-on favourites, an opinion not shared by the confident Kyles team. Neither the team, officials, nor supporters were surprised at the end with Kyles winning by three goals to one – a result that will live on in the annals of shinty.

So much for past successes, but what about Kyles Athletic today? Yes, there are criticisms to be heard and to me they are primarily threefold.

1 Lack of communication between officials and members.

2 Lack of total commitment and dedication from some players.

3 There is a need for a supporters' club which might help with the provision of transport for away matches and could encourage direct participation in the club's activities. In this way membership could be increased and members made to feel personally involved with a great club which has a great future – and what a time 1995-96 would be to bring back more trophies!

For the past eight years Henry MacKendrick has been one of Kyles Athletic's most consistent supporters – earning the unofficial title of the club's travelling padre. Not many clubs have one.

the bakehouse, Tighnabruaich, between the wars

Kyles Athletic shinty team 1930–31
the line-up contains John Olding and Alan MacFadyen recalled in the
Sorley MacLean memoir opposite. Archie Currie and Duncan Currie are
the two players at the front

ONE KYLES GAME 1933-34

Sorley MacLean

In the twenties, while I was in school in Raasay and later in Portree, I heard much about shinty. Especially in the *Oban Times* about the Glasgow Skye team. Among other things it was reported that in one game there were four of my Nicolson uncles in the Skye side and four Nicolson brothers in the Kyles team.

There was, about the mid-twenties, a very long description of a Kyles-Glasgow Skye game, when Kyles beat Skye very narrowly, the only goal of the match being scored by a Kyles player called MacKenzie. I ought to have remembered that in 1933-34, when I was playing full-back for Edinburgh Camanachd with a man from Kyles called Willie MacKenzie, who worked in the Botanic Gardens. His brother, who was called Duncan, I think, was also in the team, and they were two of the best players in the Camanachd, and very likeable men.

In 1933-34 Edinburgh Camanachd was revived after its pre-1914 lapse. We won the Southern League and the Skeabost Horn and reached the final of the Celtic Cup, in which we were beaten by Inveraray.

Before that we were knocked out of the Scottish Cup by Kyles. The Kyles team that beat us was rather unusual. Their centre, Archie Weir, the Biorach, was not playing, and their goalie was the 'veteran' Hugh Nicolson, a very tall, broad and lean man, who had been a great heavy athlete. Their famous goalie, Donald MacFadyen, was playing half-forward, and that too effectively for our defence. Their two full forwards were John Olding and Alan MacFadyen, who had

77

been a great half-back. We did have a good team with the two Mackenzies, and among our forwards the brilliant Ellis Stuart from Laggan, and Sandy Bartlett, well known as one of the Caberfeidh 'stars' when Caberfeidh were in their hey-day, before the Second World War. I could see that day that Ellis Stuart, left half-forward, was less than his usual brilliant self, being closely marked by one of the Curries.

Of course, at the full-back position I could not see very well what was happening to our forwards, or even to the two centre lines.

I don't know if there was a MacRae in the Kyles team, but then I don't remember who were the Kyles centre line and backs, nor do I remember our own centre line except MacKenzie. I don't think I knew then that the Kyles MacRaes were sons, grandsons and great grandsons of Alexander MacRae from Strathcarron, who was Free Presbyterian minister of Portree (Braes being part of his parish) until 1918, when he left to join the Free Church. He had first gone to Maryburgh, near Dingwall, but had retired to Kyles. It was said in Braes and Portree that MacRae was so greatly loved by his congregation that they would all have followed him had it not been for one elder, who was determined and influential, with many relatives. My grandfather talked of MacRae with great affection and respect.

Willie MacKenzie captained Kyles in 1928. He died in October 1995, aged 91 – and as The Times obituary made clear, was better known to the outside world as Bill, the horticulturalist. In 1968 he discovered a 'vigorous seedling clematis' at the Waterperry Horticultural School in Oxfordshire. It was propagated and named *Clematis "Bill MacKenzie"*. "William Gregor MacKenzie was born in the head gardener's cottage on the Balliemore Estate, on Loch Fyne in Argyllshire," said the obituary, "and he became interested in plants and gardening as a child. In 1928 he began his studies at the Royal Botanic Garden, but eventually moved south to beome curator of the Chelsea Physic Garden from 1946 to 1973."

Donald Macrae, winning captain 1927 with his son Alistair, winning captain 1962 – Sorley Maclean cites (opposite) the Macrae lineage.

"Boys are more easily hurt than we were," writes Duncan 'Bunks' Currie.
He is pictured here in a school shinty group (back row, right)

RECOLLECTIONS

— A FEW OF MANY

Duncan ('Bunks') Currie

As boys we played shinty all the time! Mother's only problem was getting us in at night – even as it grew dark we would tie a white hankie round the ball so that we could see to keep playing. A neighbour came out to the back road one night – we were making so much noise they thought it was the tinkers fighting!

Many's a 'green' in the Kyles never needed the grass cut, so much shinty was played. No one had money, but we were fit, strong and healthy, nourished with the best that the land, sea and air could provide.

Nothing was bought for shinty. We made our own sticks. I have a photo of a school team travelling to play in Rothesay, and you'll see all the homemade camans. We would always have an eye open for a good straight 'cass' – the Duin wood was a great source. And whenever we watched a Kyles game, we'd keep an eye and ear alert for a stick breaking – then there was a race to get hold of the broken 'bass'. This would be spliced – we were lucky with the boat-builders in the yard who were always ready to help if we couldn't manage ourselves. Even then the camans were gey easily broken.

There was never need for coaching – we practised day and night, including schooldays. There was a right row when one headmaster arrived who was only interested in football – we made some noise until he gave in and the shinty resumed. Mind you, his first day in the playground and one of the lads nearly lamed him with his caman

– it must have been a month before he ventured out at playtime again! We had some great games between the local schools – real rivalry.

We never had 'heroes'. I enjoyed watching Alan McLean from Kames playing, though he never got into the Kyles team.

I first played for the Kyles when I was sixteen. The sailing season tied in well with the shinty. We would leave to join the yacht in April through until September, then return home. The Camanachd Cup final would be played the first week in April, the Celtic Cup shortly after, so all the major competitions would be finalised before we left. In the winter we usually got a job labouring with John MacKellar, builders.

The most memorable game for me was, I think, the Camanachd Cup final in 1935 between Kyles and Caberfeidh. The Caberfeidh boys thought themselves 'cocks o' the north'. Their team, averaging thirteen stone a man was made up of fine, strong men. Both my brothers were playing in this game, and to this day people up north still talk of the game Pat played up forward – he was outstanding. My cousin Peter and myself played halfback, and Chester full-back. John Paterson came out of the juniors for that game.

The final score was 6-4 for Kyles. When we arrived home, I went into the house and got my pipes and Pat was carried shoulder high through the village to the Royal Hall for a bit of a 'do'.

I don't know if our reputation that day had anything to do with the Oban Camanchd player who told me that before a game they posted a man out of sight to count how many Curries got off the bus! I know that in one game the Oban boys came on with the instruction 'slow him (myself) down'. I had six different players on me, and even when a stick was broken across my legs I wouldn't give them the satisfaction of turning my head. Mind you, when I got home and said how tired I was, my mother's comment was, "You never got half enough."

Travelling is so much easier now. Teams used to arrive off the boat on a Saturday morning. For some of them this was their first ever time aboard a steamer. Then the walk up to the old Moss. (From Tighnabruaich Pier 2 miles, from Auchenlochan 1). There wasn't even a whin bush up there for shelter – when the wind blew you would be

Travel to games has always been interesting – for players and supporters

frozen stiff unless you kept moving all the time.

That field saw some great shinty. We would get a game going at any opportunity. I would go up with a ball in my pocket and maybe the 'Shendoys' family would be there. We'd have a hit-about and before long we'd have enough players for a game. Some of the best games were during the summer camp of the Argylls. Strangely it was always the Kames men who joined the Argylls, not the Tighnabruaich.

Even when you stop playing there's always an interest and involvement in the game. Many's the time I'd get a visit from committee, often late at night, to discuss the team or to sort out a problem.

The game has changed. You see the boys playing for the schools with great skills and potential but somehow they lose it and end up, at best, average players. They don't have the non-stop practice we had. And they're certainly more easily hurt than we were! In my day you just wouldn't lie down. But even with the influence of football being such a big TV attraction, I'm sure there will always be shinty in the Kyles.

Mrs Duncan Currie (then Jean MacCallum) remembers getting off school early and taken by bus to Millhouse, then walking the Kilfinan road to meet the bus with Pat sitting on the bonnet holding up the Cup.
Bunks's sailing career was to take him to the America's Cup, and fame, in 1937 when, on the *Endeavour*, he was feared 'lost at sea' for some days, then dubbed a modest hero by the press when he was found.

The shinty-sailing connection became more difficult for players to maintain in the 1960s and after, as the shinty seaon grew longer. Ian Irvine, verging on Olympic selection, had to choose between a number of important games and races. Dinghy sailing, then booming as windsurfing is now, proved less difficult to fit in. Chick Jamieson, crewing for Bunks's nephew Peter, won the UK Wayfarer class championship in 1966, and the more difficult UK GP14 title three years later.

Today's generation of promising shinty players, includes boys who are already in the Scottish squad for windsurfing. They include yet another Peter Currie. Chick Jamieson's son Sandy is at university on a golf scholarship.

Today's shinty club has more competition for budding sportsmen than ever. The temptations of football have always been there, especially since secondary pupils have had to go to Dunoon. But it is a similar (too similar) kind of game – Celly Paterson played for Crystal Palace during the war, and Jim Jamieson played both for Kyles and Dunoon Grammar School football team in the 1950s. The new challenge comes for individual sports, quite different in nature – in which a boy can be world champion.

We are indebted to Hugh Dan MacLennan for retrieving from the
Transactions of the Gaelic Society of Inverness, the poem opposite by a
"noted bard of Cowal, of the name of Crawford". It was written
around the 1860s. Hugh Dan notes: "Mary Anne Kennedy sang this
with harp at the MacFadyen Memorial Concert, 1993. Beautiful."
Translation by George McLennan

We have a poem by A Crawford, in English, dated 1873 dealing with
the battle that brought defeat to the MacEwens of Kilfinan.

Sheas mi car tamuill
A Crawford

Sheas mi car tamuill
Le ioghnadh gun smalan.
a'coimhead nam fearaibh
Le'n camain chruaidh ùr;
Gaoth tuath is clach-mheallain
'Gam bualadh 's na caraibh;
Bha 'chuideachd cho dannair
'S nach aithnicht' orr mùth',

Laoich chalma le 'n camain
'Gan dearbhadh 's gach bealach,
Laoich eutrom 's na caraibh
Mar cheathach nan stúc;
Car ball anns an athair
Le luathas na dealain,
'Nuair gheibh i ri spealadh
Ri talamh 'toirt cùil.

Gur bòidheach an treud iad
Air faiche le chéile,
'S iad ruith mar na fèidh
Air slèibh nam beann àrd;
A rèir cumha an fhèidhe
Bha mactalla ag èigheach;
Sud 'nis, òlaich threubhach,
Nach gèilleadh gu bràth.

O'n dualas a lean ribh
O ghuaillibh 'ur seanair,
Bhiodh cruadalachd daingeann
Nis leanachd ri 'n àl;
Ard-inntinneach fearail,
Foinnidh, fuasgailte, fallainn;
Bhiodh suathadh de 'n fhallus
Mu'n mhal' air an tràigh.

I stood awhile
A Crawford

I stood awhile
Pleasantly surprised
Watching the men
With their hard new shinty sticks;
North wind and hail
Beating on them;
So resolute a group were they
That it made no difference to them.

Sturdy heroes with their camans
In action everywhere
Heroes lightly moving
Like the mist on the peaks;
The ball in the air
With the speed of lightning
When it scythes its way
To the ground.

A fine-looking band of men
On the field together
Running like deer
On the high mountain slopes;
Like the roar of the deer
Echoes resounded;
There they are, gallant lads
Who would never yield.

From inherited character
From the shoulders of your
                    grandfathers
A strong hardiness
Would now follow on to the young
                    generation;
Proud and manly.
Hands are nimble and healthy;
The sweat of their brows
            Mingling with the sand.

Poem
A Crawford (written 1873)

A o'er hills I strayed an slowly home did go
Towards the shore I took my way and crossed the Altamore.
The night had come, the moon was bright,
the stars they twinkled clear.
This pleasant night indeed was mild tho' near the closing year.
I sat me down upon the dyke and viewed the sky around.
The sea was calm and sacred peace was brooding o'er the ground.
To have a smoke my hand I put into my jacket pouch,
Which caused a casual look from my back on the way I passed.
When to behold across the strand and rather to the sea,
Two female forms sat side by side scarce twenty yards from me.
My hair did bristle up with fear, the sweat came trickling free
As from my seat I softly stole my trembling limbs to ease.
Thinks I, my man you're done for now,
no more your pipes you'll blow.
Your fiddle strings no more you'll break or home this night you'll go,
To Auchitaggan of your march or the Clabban deep below.
Where once a peaceful honest man was taken to before.
Again I thought I none was wronged and fairies tho' they be,
A running stream I now have crossed and I have naught to fear.
So on my hands and knees I crouched, the dyke 'twixt them and me,
Till opposite to where they sat, where I could hear and see.
The young one gave a simple laugh as honest maidens do.
The old with hands around her knees was rocking to and fro.
But then she stopped and looking up full steadfast to the moon,
Her arms she folded on her breast and thus her tale began.
"O Chossack dear, what happy days along these shores I've seen,
From Kilfinan to Killal and backwards to the Glen
Where young McEwen was the heir, last of the noble line,
Who with Argyle in Covenant days could raise his hundred men.

88

With him I foraged, fought and won, for him I skipped the seas,
And what his will and wishes were, 'twas my delight to please.
But since that day that in my haste I wrecked his bonny barge
And with her lost my cantrip clues Cas-a-Moggan righ-highs charge."
She this and drew a heavy sigh I heard across the stream,
When Chossack then with tender words of sympathy began,
"These days, dear Jeanack long are past, few earth born mortal ken
And tho' I do remind the time, forget what all befell.
But as we here have time to spare, dear Jeannack tell the tale,
A truthful story new or old no one need blush to tell."
Ni mise sine's mo thruighe, you see they spoke in Gaelic.
I beg to be excused by them who never can translate it.
"McEwen he to Erin went to take his lady home.
And O she was a winsome lass besides a wealthy dame.
While he was there the men of Bute towards him acted cruel,
They came his gear and front to take and Otter House to ruin.
My hawthorn wreath I fast put on and took my Skiach wand,
And o'er the briny seas it flew McEwen for to warn.

In Ireland Jeanack urges him home, and with the help of Cas-a-Moggan's 'clue' – a matter of three knots in the sail sheets of which the third must not be undone – McEwen makes a swift passage to Loch Fyne where he loosens the forbidden knot and his gallant barge is smashed in a storm. Suppressing her rage, Jeanack urges him homeward for the next day's battle.

Meanwhile the Otter smiddy has been busy and men have been gathering from all around Kilfinan and beyond – McKellars, McEwens, Curries, Martins, Crawfords, Cattans, Lachlans and Buchanans. They march to Achnaha with McEwen and his trusty henchman, old Neil McEoch. McEwen parleys with the Butemen's leader, urging them to be gone in peace, 'lest in our just defence you justly shall be paid'. The Bodach (Buteman) leader replies:

"From Bute we came o'er fertile Isle the seas around to play.
Fighting all our study is and plundering all our trade.
Your Ballimore this day we'll take what can you do or say,
Feuch a Feuch an e mich an diabhol, you'll taste our steel today."
McEwen now with gathering hate and looks of high disdain,

The Buteman scanned form head to feet and this to him did say,
"Vain boaster of a plundering crew with words and men prepared
Your sword with mine must first be tried ere Ballimore you gain."

(They fight until . . .)

McEwen then with vengeful ire down drew his shining sword,
And deep above the Bodach's paunch with gushing force it drove.

(Once 'the gasping plunderer's life' had 'floated through the wound'
the Butemen were put to flight with much slaughter. But Jeanack's
story has a sting in the tail.)

But to my tale; my clue was lost which Cas-a-Moggan gave
And since that day her pride and spite she never yet assuaged.
With Butemen then she early and late my happy Otter pestered,
And Latterly she perished all at fatal Garav escal.
The men of Otter she subdued and plundered Ballimore.
McEwen fled to Erin's isle and back returned no more.

A BEAUTIFUL COUNTRY

– GREAT SHINTY

Sorley MacLean

I was only very young, long before I went to the School of the Clachan of Raasay, when I used to hear a song that begins:

> My fair-skinned girl of the big alluring eyes.
> Who grew up healthy and active,
> How long my step is since we parted
> At the Clachan of Glendaruel!

Even at that time the name was melodious to my ears – long before I knew that the place which had the name was beautiful and fragrant in the old traditions of the Gaels. Some years afterwards I heard how Mrs Kennedy Fraser put music on a translation of old Gaelic names in Deirdri's Farewell to Scotland:

> A dear land that land to the east,
> Alba with its wonders;
> I would not come here out of it
> If I did not come with Naoise.

Glen Massan was loved with its 'high garlic' and its 'bright branches', but the most cherished were Glen Etive in Lorne and Glen Daruel in Cowal:

> Gleann Da-ruadh – my love to every man whose heritage it is.

92

DÙTHAICH BHÒIDHEACH
– IOMAIN MHOR

Somhairle MacGill-Eain

Cha robh mi ach glé òg, fada mas deach mi a Sgoil Clachan Ratharsair,
nuair a bhithinn a' cluintinn an òrain a tha a' tòiseachadh:

> 'Mo chaileag bhian-gheal mheall-shùileach,
> A dh'fhas gu fallain fuasgailt,
> Gur trom mo cheum on dhealaich sinn
> Aig Clachan Ghlinn-da-Ruadhail'.

Eadhon aig an ám sin bha an t-ainm binn na mo chluais-fada mas robh
fhios agam gu robh an t-àite air an robh an t-ainm bòidheach agus cùbhraidh
ann an seann sheanchas nan Gaidheal. Beagan bhliadhnaichean as déidh
sin chuala mi mar a chuir NicUaraig Friseal ceòl air eadar-theangachadh
nan seann fhacal Gàidhlig ann an Soraidh Dheirdri 's i fagail na h-Albann:

> 'Ionmhainn tìr an tìr ud shear,
> Alba le a h-ìoghnaidhean;
> Cha tiginn aisde an seo
> Mura tiginn le Naoise'.

Bha Gleann Masan gràdhach le chneamh àrd 's le gheugan soilleir,' ach b'e
na h-àilleagain Gleann Eite ann an Lathurna agus Gleann Da-Ruadh ann
an Còmhal:

> 'Gleann Da Ruadh – mo chion gach fear dh'an dual

> Sweet the cuckoo's voice on bending branch
> On the mountains above Glean Da-ruadh.

Hector MacLean, the Islay man who published *Ultonian Hero Ballads* in 1892, says, "The explanation of the place-names in Deirdri's Valedictory Address to Scotland (Alba) as far as I know is that from p337 to p345 in Brown's *Memorials of Argyle-shire*.

Mr Brown is a native of Cowal himself and he seems to me to show clearly that the place-names mentioned in Deirdri's Valedictory Address to Alba are Cowal place-names.

At any rate, it is very likely, almost certain, that some of the names are from Cowal, and that the rest are from the 'beautiful land of MacCailein' as a peaceful stanza in the terrible song *MacNaughton of the Dun* puts it:

> Many a boat and ship
> Are cheerfully going
> Between Ireland of the hosts
> And the lovely land of MacCailein.

I remember that once upon a time it gave me a sort of pleasure to hear that one or two or three of the Kyles of Bute shinty players were from Glendaruel. (I think that one of them was named MacIntyre.)

But it is not Glendaruel alone that is exceedingly beautiful in Cowal, and it is not the only place in those districts to have a halo of sun or moon with the colours of songs, poems and stories.

Ewen MacColl put an added lustre on Loch Eck, and there was another man who lit the braes of that loch with a love-song to a MacLeod woman, who "was reared by the side of Loch Aic", one who would keep a man's eye during the sermon "even if St Paul were in the pulpit."

If I knew the Kyles of Bute and all Cowal better than I do, perhaps I could write far more about the traditions, songs and poems of the country. It is almost sixty years since I sailed from Gourock through the Kyles to Tarbert Loch Fyne.

Three or four years ago I went in a car through much of Cowal, but I have never seen the two sides of Loch Striven nor Glen Massan.

Is binn guth cuaich air craoibh chruim
Air a' bheinn os Gleann Da-Ruadh'.

Tha Eachann MacGill-eain, an t-Ileach a chuir a mach 'Ultonian Hero Ballads',
'Duain Curaidhean Uladh', ann an 1892, ag ràdh: 'Se am m∞neachadh as
fheàrr a rinneadh air na h-aimnean ann an "Soraidh Dheirdri, . . . fhad as
aithne dhomhsa, am fear a gheibhear o dhuilleig 337 gu 345 anns na
Memorials of Argyle le MacGille Dhuinn. Tha MacGille Dhuinn de mhuinntir
Chòmhail e fhéin, agus a réir mo bheachd-sa, tha e nochdadh gu soilleir
gur h-e ainmean á Còmhal a tha ann an Soraidh Dheirdri.'

Co-dhiù, tha e glé choltach, cha mhór cinnteach, gu bheil cuid de na
h-ainmean á Còmhal, agus gu bheil càch á cearnaidhean eile de 'dhùthaich
bhòidhich MhicCailein', mar a tha rann sèimh anns an òran uamharra
'MacNeachdainn an Dùin' ga chur:

'S iomadh bàta is long
Tha le fonn a' dol seachad
Eadar Eirinn nan slògh
Is dùthaich bhòidhich MhicCailein'.

Tha cuimhne agam, uair a bha siod, gun d'thug e seòrsa de thlachd dhomh
a chluinntinn gun robh fear no dithis no triùir de dh'iomainichean Caolais
Bhòid á Gleann Da-Ruadhail. Tha mi dhen bheachd gur h-e Mac an t-Saoir
a bha air fear dhiubh.

Ach chan e Gleann Da-Ruadhail leis fhéin a tha anabarrach bòidheach
ann an Còmhal, agus chan e an aon cheàrnaidh anns na sgìrean sin air a
bheil cearcall grèine no gealaiche le dathan nan òran is nan dàn is nan
sgeulachdan. Chuir Eóghann MacColla loinn a bharrachd air Loch Aic,
agus bha fear eile a las bruaichean an locha le òran gaoil do NicLeòid air
choireigin, a 'dh'fhàs taobh Loch Aic', té a chumadh sùil fir anns an t-
searmon 'ged bhiodh Pòl sa chùbaid'.

Na robh mise na b'eòlaiche na tha mi air Caolais Bhòid agus air
Còmhal uile dh' fhaodadh gum b'urrainn dhomh fada bharrachd a
sgrìobhadh mu sheanchas, mu bheul aithris, mu òrain na dùthcha. Tha
faisg air trì fichead bliadhna on sheòl mi á Guireig, troimh na caoil gu
Tairbeart Loch Fìne. O chionn trì no ceithir bliadhna chaidh mi ann an car
troimh mhóran de Chòmhal, ach chan fhaca mi riamh da thaobh Loch

95

I wish I could have an opinion, whether Inver Massan is 'noisy' or 'grassy' or both*. Though I have not been on either side of Loch Striven I have been where the road goes up high, about two or three miles north-east of Tigh-na-Bruaich. From that high place the view is marvellous.

In our own day there was an exceptionally fine poet, a near neighbour of the Kyles of Bute and of a great part of Cowal, one who was a poet in Gaelic, in English, in Highland English, and in Lowland Scots – George Campbell Hay, or, as he himself would say, the son of John, son of George. His boat was very near the Kyles:

> Eilean Aoidh – joyous was her roaring;
> Ardlamont – haughty was her shouting;
> Up off Inchmarnoch she sang a ditty.

* Hector MacLean translates the word as 'grassy', but Dwelly's Dictionary suggests 'noisy'. It could refer to (wild) hemlock.

Stroigheann no Gleann Masan. B'fhearr leam gum b'urrainn dhomh beachd a bhith agam, an ann fuaimneach no feurach a tha "Inbhir Mangach Masain". Ged nach robh mi air taobh seach taobh de Loch Stroigheann, bha mi far a bheil an rathad a'dol suas àrd, mu dhà no trì mìle an ear-thuath air Taigh na Bruaich. On àird sin tha an sealladh mìorbhaileach.

'Nar linn fhìn bha bàrd air leth ann, 'na nàbaidh dlùth do Chaolais Bhòid agus do roinn mhóir de Chòmhal, fear a bha 'na bhàrd an Gàidhlig, am Beurla Shasainn, ann am Beurla Ghàidhealach agus Ghallda-Deòrsa Caimbeul Hay, no, mar a chanadh e fhéin, Mac Iain Dheòrsa. Bha a bhàta glé fhaisg air na Caolais:

> 'Eilean Aoidh – bu aoibh a nuallan,
> Aird MhicLaomainn – a gaoir gum b'uaibhreach,
> Os cionn na h-Innse sheinn i duanag.'

Celly Paterson during World War II

TIGHNABRUAICH

AND THE SECOND WORLD WAR

Alan C Millar

While there was no enemy action in and around the Kyles of Bute
the area did not go unscathed by war. In one way it was relatively
isolated with road access only along Loch Fyneside. On the other
hand, most communications had always been by sea and because of
the antisubmarine boom across the firth from Dunoon to Inverkip
the grey-painted MacBrayne mailboat Lochfyne left daily for five
years from Wemyss Bay rather than Gourock. Throughout the war
there was a continuous and reliable daily service as far as Ardrishaig.

In 1938 the fear of Luftwaffe bombing had prompted the
appointment everywhere of Air Raid Wardens and even in
Tighnabruaich Air Raid Shelters were established. But the area's
particular role inthe three years following the Dunkirk evacuation in
1940 was the provision of military training areas in preparation for
the invasion of Europe. This reached its climax from the autumn of
1943 until early summer of 1944 when Kilfinan parish's population
was swollen tenfold. Of course, Tighnabruaich, like all Highland
communities, was emotionally devastated by the loss into captivity
of the 51st (Highland) Division at St Valery in the spring of 1940.

Before the arrival of exhausted and battle-weary troops
evacuated from Dunkirk Tighnabruaich housed about 250 Polish
soldiers. They were followed by French Canadians and English
soldiers from the East Midlands whose formation, however, included
a battalion of Scots Guards. Americans were warmly welcomed and

the US 6th Ranger Battalion has commemorated its months in Cowal with a plaque in the Kames Recreation Hall; in recent years several veterans have returned on holiday.

While troops were, of course, billetted in private houses throughout the village special military accommodation had to be quickly built, mostly huts erected on concrete bases on what is now the shinty field with NAAFI canteens set up in Kames, Auchenlochan and Tighnabruaich. While Special Forces and the Royal Navy concentrated their training on upper and lower Loch Fyne, the Kerry Kyle was the particular scene for amphibious units preparing for D Day. The 'tank landing strip' at Kames was built by Royal Engineers in the space of about a fortnight in 1943 to accommodate tracked fighting vehicles which practised assaults along both the west shore of the Kyle and on to the beach at Ostal Bay. Local people grew used to convoys of military vehicles.

The civilian population also grew with the first influx of evacuees soon after war's outbreak. More than a hundred children, also pregnant women, arrived in the village from Clydebank. However, the quiet of Argyll was so totally different from the city that only a few of the evacuees stayed for long. In 1941 there were more arrivals following enemy bombing of Glasgow, Clydebank, and Greenock. Space had to be found over two years for ninety extra schoolchildren.

For about nine months most of Kilfinan Parish was a Restricted Area. Only those whose families lived there could visit it and for a while the Ardlamont peninsula from Millhouse to Point Farm was cleared to permit live firing. The occupants of Carry, Clachan and Whinbank were given a week's notice and warned that their removal could be for a week, a month, all summer, or for the duration of the war. In the event they got back for a short while by late 1943. By the end of that summer all Ardlamont was again evacuated and no one was allowed home until 1946.

Sheep and cattle were moved well inland but during intervals between firing when the red flags were lowered farmers were able to return briefly to tend crops. There was quite substantial damage to some property. Ammunition dumped by Italian Prisoners of War was stored in huts in the woods between Blair's Ferry and Whinbank

local defence volunteers on parade in Tighnabruaich, World War II;
troops were also billeted in the village for invasion training

and later parties of these prisoners were used to help in making safe unexploded devices, a job that was not completed until Royal Engineer Bomb Disposal parties had cleared the area in 1948.

Ostal Bay, deemed particularly suitable for practice landings, was the scene of at least one major accident when it appears that one or more US tanks was lost between leaving a landing craft and getting ashore. Infantry training with live ammunition took its toll and while figures for casualties are unclear it seems that there may have been more than forty fatalities. Certainly, on one day twelve coffins were loaded on to *The Lochfyne* at Tighnabruaich Pier.

For almost a year Tighnabruaich House became a military hospital staffed jointly by British and American military medical services. Caladh Castle requisitioned early in the war by the Royal Navy became a 'stone frigate'. HMS *James Cook*, a navigation school. The Royal Navy also used the Kyles for midget submarine training. While the Admiralty were good tenants who did little damage to Caladh the castle was retained by the Government after the Navy left as a possible home for European displaced persons who, in the event, never arrived and because its structure was badly neglected while it lay empty it was in such poor repair by 1945 that it was demolished by Territorial Army Engineers about 1960.

After the departure of fighting units in 1944 for the Normandy beaches there was an increase in the number of Italian Prtisoners of War all accommodated in the requisitioned Royal Hotel and in quickly built hutted accommodation nearby. A relic of their stay is the terrazo floor still to be seen on the hotel's doorstep.

On one level the price paid was less than elsewhere. While all men and women of military age not in reserved occupations were, of course, in uniform, the Kilfinan Parish war memorial records only six names, many fewer lost than the forty-nine killed in the slaughter of World War I.

(Information culled from a variety of sources, mostly the memories of those who spent their childhood in the village during the war; thanks also to the Argyll and Bute Council Archivist)

WARTIME ECHO

Joe Donachie

Before returning home from a scholarship visit to Italy I visited the small coastal resort of Torvianica, twenty miles south of Rome. In the hotel I found myself invited, as a foreign visitor, to sit at the family table in the dining room. During conversation I was asked in broken English by the proprietor if I was English.

"No, no, I am Scottish," I said in Italian. (I knew enough then.)

He then asked if I know a place called Tighnabruaich!!!

Well – when I picked myself up from the floor – I quietly explained that I lived there. And he in turn explained that he had been a prisoner of war in the Royal Hotel – and had made the mosaic at the front door (which is still there to this day).

a slimline Joe falling from chair

Joe Donachie is a retired art teacher. In 1962 he won the Newbury prize as best student at Glasgow School of Art. He went to Italy in 1960, on a Royal Scottish Academy scholarship.

WHITE APRON DAYS

1946 Kyles 50 years old.

(1953 Lovat 4, Kyles 1 at Ft William after 2-2, Oban. 1955 Newtonmore
    5, Kyles 2, Glasgow)

1956 Kyles 4, Kilmallie 1, Oban. Suez crisis, Hungarian uprising, first
    CND Aldermaston march, rock 'n' roll, Melbourne Olympics.

(1957 Newtonmore 3, Kyles 1, Spean Bridge; 1959 Newtonmore 7,
    Kyles 3, Glasgow)

1962 Kyles 3, Kilmallie 1, Inverness. Eichmann hanged, Telstar
    launched, Rod Laver wins tennis grand slam, Arnold Palmer's
    second British Open in a row, Marilyn Monroe dies.

1965 Kyles 4, Kilmallie 1, Oban. Lyndon Johnson inaugurated US
    President – race riots, anti-Vietnam protests, Malcolm X shot,
    civil rights marches, Radio Caroline established, Jim Clark
    world motor-racing champion.

1966 Kyles 3, Newtonmore 2, Inverness. Kyles win every competition
    entered. Indira Ghandi Prime Minister of India, Henry Cooper
    loses two title fights to Cassius Clay, England win World Cup
    (football), Walt Disney dies.

1968 Kyles 2, Kingussie 1, Oban, after 3-3 Fort William. Martin Luther
    King, Bobby Kennedy assassinated, Nixon elected US
    president, Jim Clark killed, Jacqui Kennedy marries Onassis,
    Russians invade Czechoslovakia, civil rights marches in
    N Ireland, Olympic Games, Mexico.

1969 Kyles 3, Kilmallie 1, Oban. Army sent to N Ireland, Rocky
    Marciano dies, Rod Laver wins second grand slam, first men
    on the moon.

(1970, 1971, Newtonmore 7, Kyles 1, at Kingussie, Inverness)

Tally at 1971 (Kyles 75 years old) Newtonmore 19, Kyles 15.
Celtic Cup 1954, 56, 60, 63, 65, 66, 67, 70;
MacAulay Cup 1956, 58, 61, 66, 71;
Sutherland 1961;
Dunn Cup 1950, 51, 61, 62, 65, 66, 68.

1974 Kyles 4, Kingussie 1, Oban. Sam Goldwyn dies, Heath resigns,
Wilson wins two elections, Muhammad Ali beats George
Foreman to regain heavyweight championship, W Germany
win World cup (football)

(1975 Newtonmore 1, Kyles 0), Ft William, after 3-3, Kingussie)

1976 Kyles 4, Newtonmore 2, Inverness. Montgomery, Mao die,
Wilson resigns, Vietnam war ends, Concorde's first trans-
atlantic supersonic services, Montreal Olympics.

(1977,78,79, Newtonmore beat Kyles 5-3, 3-2. 4-3)

1980 Kyles 6, Newtonmore 5, Kingussie. Rhodesia becomes
Zimbabwe, Peter Sellers dies, JR 'shot', Mt St Helens erupts,
Borg wins fifth successive Wimbledon, Iraq-Iran war starts,
Reagan becomes president, Moscow Olympics.

1983 Kyles 3, Strachur 2, at Ft William – first 'open draw' final.
Thatcher re-elected, Borg retires, Richard Noble's *Thrust II* does
633.6 mph, Australia wins America's Cup.

1994 Kyles 3, Fort William 1, Inverness. Lilliehammer Olympics, wars
in Rwanda, fomer Yugoslavia, former Soviet Union. Promise
of peace in Israel and Ireland.

Tally at 1996: Kyles 100 years – Newtonmore 28, Kyles 20,
Kingussie 12.
Celtic Cup 76, 77, 79, 81, 83, 84, 86;
MacAulay 71, 72, 77, 78, 89;
Sutherland 75,80,87;
National League, 1986.
Dunn 72, 73, 74, 75, 77, 78, 79, 80, 81 (shared with Oban Celtic), 83,
84, 85, 96, 87, 88.

My first memories of shinty (writes Iain Thorburn) are not of glory, but of devastating defeats – a 9-1 pasting for Tighnabruaich at the hands of Millhouse (who played in blue and white hoops) and a 10-2 hammering for Kyles, at home to Ballachulish. I may have got the games mixed up, but the heart-sinking scorelines have stuck.

Around about the same time – the first couple of years after the war, before I emigrated from Tighnabruaich to Kames – I got a real shinty for Christmas, made by a neighbour, Jimmy Warden. I can still smell the varnish and the tape. I remember too, another neighbour, Maitland Black, who lost no opportunity in telling us that in shinty, reality was called Newtonmore. (Newtonmore contested the first five finals after World War II, winning four, but it was to be some years before I found out just what he meant – that other team in blue-and-white hoops beat Kyles in the first three finals I attended.)

A few years ago, I visited Newtonmore Primary School on business, and the head, Donald MacDonald, had primed one of the classes to welcome me with a choral recitation of a poem celebrating one of these victories. It occurred to me then that while shinty is on the curriculum at Tighnabruaich, perhaps coaching ought to be backed up with lessons in the lore of the club. Newtonmore's bards have had plenty to celebrate in the post-war years, including, twice, the most sickening scoreline of my adult years – 7-1.

If this seems an odd way to celebrate a centenary, well we are not here to bury Kyles, and there is nothing more tedious or less convincing than an extended eulogy. Sure, Kyles have been a successful shinty club, but a club's success and esteem is measured against that of others, and in the respect they earn from their rivals.

That is why in this celebratory publication we have looked outside the district and to the wider world of shinty for an appreciation of Kyles Athletic's achievements. Kyles and Newton-more have a respect for one another that is reflected in their songs, and that is worth recording.

So is the fact that success does not come easily. The great players of the past were not invincible. Kyles have produced good teams and good players who have never laid a hand on the Camanachd Cup. This is not said to comfort the present team but to set them and their successors a realistic target. Kyles Athletic in its first fifty years was the most successful club in Scotland, on the only measure that mattered. Since the first half century included two world wars, the teams in the second fifty years have played more games, and won more finals than their predecessors – but the club is now only the second most successful in Scotland. It is up to the present and future teams to do better – and since the Camanachd Association is as slavish as ever in following wherever football leads, the measure of success in the next century will sooner or later cease to be the Camanachd Cup and become the National League. Unless the Association have overreached themselves, this is a development Kyles cannot ignore for long – the club will have to acquire new priorities, and reacquire some lost habits, if the next centenary celebration is not to be a wake.

The first final I remember was in 1953, which I heard on the wireless. Lovat players remember the drawn game at Oban for the rain – and the advantage it gave to Kyles, whom they thought were all fishermen. Indeed, as I recall, the commentator – a Canadian ice-hockey man, I believe, said he was watching it through the buttonhole of his coat.

By this time I was a Kames boy, learning what shinty was all about from the likes of Donnie MacNiven, Ally Turner and Norman Crowe – whose Granpa MacDougall used to steam shinties into the bend. Alistair Chambers ran the BB. My neighbour, Martin "Rattler" Salisbury had a silver-mounted shinty on his wall. And at Sammy Morrison's we waited for our haircuts enthralled by the talk among our heroes in the then senior team. Sammy, a well-travelled man with a touch of the Blarney, was a keen shinty fan, and it was there that I started to hear about the great men of the pre-war days – especially the MacFadyens.

Turner is a name that echoes through Kyles second fifty years as Nicolson did in the first – above Peter, Charlie and Scott in 1976

I still think my greatest moment in shinty was when Donnie MacNiven picked me for his Ainsworth Medal team. But soon after, Donnie took his matchless talent to Glasgow, and devoted it to Mid-Argyll, for whom his young brother Kenny was also a star. His older brother Ackie, however, remained a Kyles stalwart, almost no matter how far away his work took him. Norman Crowe and Ally Turner also played for Kyles, but Norman was lost to Glasgow Police, to whom he devoted his best years. Ally was lost to National Service, and then to London. There was a time when I thought Kyles' biggest contribution to the game was its export of players to Mid-Argyll – most notably perhaps the two MacNivens, the two Turners, John Rae and 'Tumshie', and, in his college years, Barney Crawford.

Turner is a name that echoes through Kyles second fifty years as Nicolson did in the first. Ally was the first of six brothers: Jock was lost to the police, but Scott, Peter, Chick (before he, too, joined up) and Donald were all Kyles players. And all, except Ally, met on the shinty field when Kyles played Strathclyde Police. (MacTurnor, incidentally, is one of the names taken by the Lamont brothers who – true to the clan's genius for picking the wrong side, offended Robert III by killing three lairds who were his guests on Bute. The Lamonts had supported John Balliol against Robert the Bruce.)

Ally, who won Camanachd and Celtic honours, told me recently that the best team he ever played in was the school team that was soundly beaten by Kingussie in the MacPherson Cup in 1954: Tom Nicolson, Charles Black, Duncan Munro, Norman Crowe, Iain Irvine, Robbie Edgar, Donnie MacNiven, Billy Crawford, Ally Turner, Gordon MacLellan, Jim Jamieson, and Jamie Tallach. I was at that game, and also in the fifties saw two Camanachd finals at Glasgow and one at Spean Bridge which Kyles lost to guess who – but I did not see the 1956 final, when Neil Black lifted the Cup. This was a very important breakthrough, and a fitting reward for players such as Alistair Chambers, Alistair Irvine, Tommy Nicolson, and Celly Paterson – not to mention Captain Duncan MacRae.

Equally important, by then shinty was thriving in school, thanks to Graham Cross, a Borderer who had arrived knowing nothing of the game. Before that, shinty had not been exactly encouraged in the playground. It quickly became the scene of titanic struggles featuring Iain Irvine and Donnie MacNiven, who were unfortunately the only two third year members of the 1954 MacPherson Cup side.

That trophy was to be won two years in a row by the next generation of Graham's boys – including Allan Simpson, Chic Jamieson, Roddy Carswell and Ginger MacNeill. Graham's next, and last crop, included Stuart Davidson, Jock Turner, Davie MacCallum, Russell Thorburn, Neil Blair, and Scott Turner, all future Camanachd winners, unless they went away. Graham went away to be head at Lochgilphead – and foster shinty there – as Tighnabruaich School was reduced in stages to primary status. I too went away and for one reason or another missed their triumphs of the early sixties. It was not until 1965 that I saw Kyles win the cup.

I missed the great 1966 final, in what was a great year for Kyles, but I remember the Kilmallie games for the great interplay between Jim Jamieson and Tom Nicolson – and the final against Kingussie in which my brother scored the winning goal. (In 1974 he was to captain the winning team against the same opposition).

In these days the most exciting and important games were the semi-finals, usually at Inveraray, usually close-run things between Kyles and Oban Celtic or Glasgow Mid-Argyll. The Celtic Cup was more difficult to win than the Camanachd, and an open draw at that time would have produced a succession of all-South finals.

On the junior front, I missed the 1961 final described by John MacKenzie, and in 1964, along with Kruschev's son and Sir Fitzroy MacLean, saw Kyles go down to Boleskine at Strachur. But I was at Oban in 1975 when Kyles beat Newtonmore 6-3, with Colin MacColl outstanding at centre. I missed the 1980 triumph against Kingussie, but in 1987 saw the riveting final at Taynuilt which ended 7-5 to Kyles against Glenurquhart after extra time. Peter Mobeck scored an 'impossible' goal from what seemed to be the bye-line, and Peter Briggs was superb in the middle.

As is often the case, not just in shinty and not just with Kyles, a successful team can go over the hill imperceptibly, and in 1970 and 71 Newtonmore were waiting to drive that lesson home. But perhaps the most significant aspect of these two disasters was that Kyles were

111

back only three years later, and stayed there or thereabouts for ten years. For me the most memorable game of the seventies, among many, was the Inverness final against Newtonmore in 1976, which I still rate the best game I have ever seen, though the 6-5 against the same team in 1980 was perhaps more exciting. Neil Blair won the man of the match award in the first for his half-back display – and scored the winner in the second from second forward, when George 'Squire' Nicolson was man of the match. That era is described, as seen through more impartial eyes, by Douglas Lowe.

It was the seventies that brought the promise of industry to replace, at last, the Powderworks. But the Portavadie oil-rig production yard turned out to be a massive waste of public money, producing a village that was never occupied and a huge hole in the ground that never smelt an order, let alone built a platform. And none of the promises of compensation and help for local amenities was fulfilled.

In the eighties there was the great open draw final against Strachur in 1983, when as we saw it in Cowal the wheels fell off the North shinty bandwagon. The Cup could easily have been Strachur's that year, but Barney Crawford decided otherwise.

Kyles' solitary league cup win, in 1986, when Tom Whyte starred in a sparsely attended, rain-soaked final at Inverness against Kingussie – was as satisfying, in its way, as the MacAulay victory in 1989 that ended Kingussie's unbeaten run. That was undoubtedly James MacDonald's game. His career was to be cut short by illness.

But in truth there was not much to savour during the Camanachd Cup wilderness years, which ended in 1994 with a sweet victory against the bookies' and commentators' favourites, Fort William. That has to be the game of the nineties – so far. Man of the match was Andy Irvine, and Neil Nicolson netted a vital penalty – thus do the names of the club's founders echo down the years.

Cup winning teams from the 1960s ...

The 1962 winners, Tom Nicolson, Roddie Carswell, Jim Jamieson, Charles Black, Alistair Macrae (captain), Ian Irvine, Chic Jamieson, Alistair Chambers, Bobby Nicolson, Allan Simpson and Alistair McNiven

the 1970s . . .

The 1976 Camanachd Cup winners, fronted by George Nicolson (captain, holding trophy) and Neil Blair (man of the match)

and the 1990s

The team that ended the Camanachd Cup wilderness years in 1994 with a
sweet victory against the bookies' and commentators' favourites, Fort
William
back
Colin MacColl, Jamie Strickland, Donald MacPhail, Ronnie MacVicar,
Norman MacDonald, Andy Irvine, Kenny MacDonald, Iain Taylor,
Ally Wren, Andy MacDonald, Robert Baxter, Scott Turner, John Paterson
front
Neil Nicolson, Donald Macrae, Iain Macrae, Peter Mobeck, David Taylor,
Fraser MacDonald, Kenny Allan, Tom Whyte

115

THE
GLASGOW CELTIC SOCIETY CUP

John MacLeod (contd)

After the second World War the competition for the Celtic Cup resumed in season 1946-47, but the name of Kyles Athletic does not appear on the Cup until 1954, when, led by A Chambers, they inflicted a 5-1 defeat on Glasgow Mid Argyll, with whom an intense rivalry developed in this particular competition.

Two years later, a replayed match with Mid Argyll resulted in a 1-1 draw but, by virtue of having forced three corners to their opponents one, Kyles, under the captaincy of N Black, were awarded the trophy.

Glasgow Mid Argyll, then Cup-holders, were again the victims on 21 May 1960, when I Irvine led the team which won a high-scoring, close encounter by 6-5.

In 1963, T Nicolson captained the team which won the Cup. They lost in the final of 1964 to Glasgow Mid Argyll but gained their revenge the following year when J Jamieson led them to a convincing 5-0 win. This began a three year domination of the Celtic Cup. In 1966, C Jamieson emulated his brother by captaining a Cup-winning team. Bute were beaten 6-1. In 1967, there was a much closer contest. R Carswell was captain when Mid Argyll were beaten by 3-2 in "one of the best finals seen in recent years". (Glasgow Celtic Society minutes, 30 August, 1967)

117

There was another victory in the final of the 1970 competition when S Davidson was club captain.

In 1975, Kyles Athletic and Inveraray, who were the Cup-holders, reached the final and were informed in a letter dated 22 April of the arrangements for the final to be played in Glasgow on 31 May and that playing it outwith Glasgow in the previous year had been "an error" and was not "according to the constitution of the Society."

Both clubs replied in similar terms, in letters dated 29 April, that they would be willing to play in Glasgow, but only on condition that all travel and meals' expenses be borne by the Society. Failing this, both clubs suggested Strachur as a venue. These letters were considered at a meeting of the Directors of the Society on 5 May and, on 6 May, a reply was sent to the clubs reaffirming Glasgow as the venue and stating that the Society could not undertake to meet the expenses of the participants. To allow preparations for the final to proceed, written confirmation that they were "agreeable to playing in Glasgow on the above conditions" was requested by 14 May. (Correspondence and minutes of meetings of the Glasgow Celtic Society, April/May 1975)

Neither club replied by the stipulated date – neither had the courtesy to reply at all – and the Cup was withheld for that year.

When invitations were sent to clubs for the 1975-76 competition, the rules, as laid down in the constitution of the Society, were reiterated, and the competition proceeded smoothly. Kyles Athletic were the winners, under the captaincy of G Nicolson, and again the next year under D MacNeil.

When the Centenary Final was played on 23 June 1979 it was perhaps appropriate that Kyles Athletic, with a record of twenty two wins to their credit, should be contesting the final. The *Glasgow Herald* match report stated that their opponents, Oban Camanachd, "took an early two-goal lead . . . before Kyles had a chance to settle." Before half-time, "Duncan MacVicar pulled one back with a thundering shot from thirty yards into the roof of the net." An own-goal by Oban Camanachd made it 2-2 before "Kyles captain, Chic Turner, scored the winner after brother Scott slipped a free-hit to him."

Kyles had made it twenty three wins in the seventy five years for which it had been played and it must be remembered that there had been eight competitions before Kyles became involved, so making the club's record more impressive.

Note:
Since the Centenary Final, Kyles have had only three more wins, in 1983, 1984, and 1986 (R Irvine, D MacVicar and D Macrae, captains)

THE KYLES

THE REFEREE'S TALE

G Y Slater

I was asked to write a humorous account of my shinty visits to the
'Hallowed Kyles' but first let me pay my own tribute to some of the
people who helped me in the early days and have made their own
special contribution to to the game, both on and off the field.

Jimmy Nicolson was President of Kyles when I was introduced
to the game as a referee. He always gave me that special treatment.
He was thoughtful both to his own boys, as he called them, and to
visiting teams, and his treament of referees was no different, win or
lose. Big Jimmy never sought to put blame on anyone and if Kyles
lost he would say, "Better luck next time," and everyone knew what
he meant.

Celly Paterson will find his own special place in the game. Shinty
is the poorer for his passing and no one has quite filled the vacancy
caused by his untimely death. Captain Duncan MacRae of Ballimore,
a past Chief of the Camanachd Association, was a most generous
benefactor to the club. His care for visitors to Kyles was legendary
and few left the parish without sampling his kindness. Neil Paterson
and his good lady at Drum Farm were others who showed
consideration to shinty travellers, whether it was a couple in a car or
a whole bus load it made little difference to the residents at Drum –
no matter what time of day or night they called.

Shinty has regrettably changed in recent times. Winning seems
to have become a top priority with everything going to the winners
and runners-up being of little consequence. Perhaps this has always
been the case, but at past Cup Finals receptions the need to get home

with the trophy wasn't so urgent – indeed after winning the Camanachd Cup Kyles stayed overnight in their Inverness hotel sharing the honour with a strong travelling support.

My remit, however, is not to put right the many wrongs of our game, but rather to recall some of the lighter moments of play as they affected the 'wee' man in the middle. I remember one of my earlier games at Tighnabruaich, when Kyles were hosts to Lochfyneside. Dunkie Luke got the better of Winston Nicolson early on, rounded the powerful farmer, and sent the ball into the roof of the net. Winston was at the centre before I was, protesting, "Slater, that was no goal."

"Was it not?" I replied. "Just you read tomorrow's *Sunday Post* and you'll see it was a goal all right."

Neil Galbraith gave yeoman service in the Kyles colours, but he didn't possess the best of humour. I remember pulling him up for tackling from behind and I informed him he would have to watch his fouling.

He looked at me and said, "Slater, you couldn't pick out a foul at a hen show."

When a player is injured the first thing you do is assure him that his injury isn't serious, but that wasn't the way of Donny Whyte, who was respected for his economy with words. Jim Felgate of Oban Camanachd was injured high on his forehead in a game I was in charge of at Kyles. The players quickly gathered round and as the visiting trainer was attending him his team mates were assuring him that despite the blood the wound wouldn't need a stitch.

Enter Donny Whyte.

After surveying the scene he agreed with the Oban players. "Aye, you're right enough, it's a hem it needs."

Such incidents recall happy times I spent in the Tighnabruaich area, and I hope all will rejoice with me when Kyles are once again back leading the pack. That's where they belong, but to reclaim their territory much needs to be done both within and without the club.

Nothing is achieved in the game if you lack dedication. Kyles have never been short of this commodity in the past, and they certainly don't lack it at the moment. Now is time to recharge the batteries, bring the player pool up to acceptable numbers and win your place on the playing field. If you are successful there, then shinty officials may come round to your way of thinking. I wish the club all the best for the next hundred years.

George, or 'G Y' Slater as he is known throughout the game, was a referee for many years – and afterwards for many more reported and commented on shinty in the *Oban Times*.

THE KYLES

A LIGHT ON THE ROAD

John A Paterson

From my first memory, shinty has played a large part in my life. We used to rip up old jerseys for John Mackellar to make shinty balls and then get one for Christmas, and at other times we would cut old sticks from the hedge or from any tree that looked likely.

In Drum, Sunday lunch was the time that the Saturday game was replayed and every detail of the school, junior and senior games discussed.

Growing up with a family who could not see past shinty and who had a bit of flat ground outside meant that the wee field held many hard-fought battles with the Youngs, Jimmy Mathieson, Whaler, Winston, Mary, the Fergusons and anyone who wanted to play. Drum was a stopping-off place too, for many teams on their way back from Tighnabruaich after a game.

Usually on a Saturday night after a Kyles home game and a meal given by Captain Duncan, my father would get a lift home from the visiting team and invite them in for a cup of tea or a wee dram with the words, "Betty won't mind." The only time I heard my mother say it was a bit much was after a North Argyll v South Argyll match and a fifty four seater busload came in for tea and a dram! All the top names in shinty from Oban were there – Leslie Grout, Jock Douglas, Jimmy Mitchell. They all stayed until midnight and left after an Oban Celtic player had visited the byre and turned the wrong way as he came out in the dark. No one was aware of this until he fell headlong through the closed window of the front room, saying he could not find the door.

Often 'the light on the road' would attract Inveraray players and with Skinner and Duncan MacKay a ceilidh would start and continue until the small hours. One night they left and travelled four miles up the road thinking one of the team was very quiet in the dark. In fact, they had to return to Drum to find this 'quiet man' sound asleep at the fireplace. They had all walked past him to leave the house.

'The light on the road' must have shone brightly the night the Bute team missed the ferry and all came to stay until morning. It was not the Colintraive–Rhubodach vessel they missed but the Wemyss Bay boat and they drove round the road to Drum for a cup of tea.

In the Deerstalker (now Glenmorangie) Shield a north team would be invited to play. Newtonmore visited and were booked into Kames Hotel. However the next morning fourteen were sleeping on Drum floors, beds, chairs etc. One player who had shared a bed with four team-mates awoke to see a strange head next to him in the dusk. He shot out of bed, put on his shoes and walked away down the road. After he had gone a hundred yards, he realised he was in Kilfinan, not Newtonmore.

Before accusations of bias are made, I must also say that Kingussie often stayed in the area and several big names had to be spoon-fed at Drum. For them too, it was a case of lights out on the Kilfinan road.

Most homeward bound teams stopped at Drum and we all have fond memories of Mid-Argyll with the Giosh, the Geyman and Jimmy Black all telling their stories in the front room. Drum was in a good place as the first stop after Tighnabruaich or the last stop before home for a returning Kyles team. "Toasted cheese at Drum!" was a cry often heard as cars left the Creggans or St Catherine's for another chance to replay the match.

After one away game a few of the boys thought they would buy Mother chocolates, bread and cheese to thank her for all the times they had stopped. That night they ate all they had brought plus all that was in the house as well. The chocolates disappeared too!

In June 1969 the new road opened and that was the end of the need to pass Drum. In late August of that year Glasgow Police were playing at the Kyles. I had played in that game and was getting ready to go back to Tighnabruaich when I met the police bus bringing Neil Drum home, so they had to come in for a cup of tea or a wee dram after being again told, "Betty won't mind." Glasgow Police had the last team bus to stop at Drum as dad died six weeks after that.

The memories will live on but "the light on the road" is now out. The long walk out the passage in Drum left its mark on everyone who called.

THE KYLES

ALISTAIR ARTHUR CHAMBERS

Ronnie MacFarlane

Not for a moment did it ever dawn on Arthur and Jessie Chambers that their fifth child, Alistair, born on the 26th of October 1926 would one day become recognised as the supreme gentleman of shinty by all his peers throughout the shinty world. Whenever shinty men pause to discuss our ancient game – calling as it does for talent, skill and above all sportsmanship, then the name that is most likely to come up in the conversation is that of Alistair Chambers.

At the age of seventeen Alistair joined the Army and for the next seven years he saw active service with the famous Parachute Regiment, being wounded in action. His innate modesty prevented any great details of his service being disclosed but information to hand suggests that he had had what is termed "a distinguished war".

When he was demobilised Alistair returned to his first love, shinty, and made his debut in the Kyles team in 1952 in the position he was to make his own – centre. His first game was against Oban Celtic in Oban and, thanks to repeated warnings from a local worthy, he had convinced himself that his prospective opponent was at least seven feet tall with a temper to match. To his surprise, he found the opponent in question was an ordinary individual with a normal physique – a man later to become one of his best friends in shinty.

During his playing career honours galore fell to him. Every known available medal found its way into his collection. Camanachd, Celtic, MacAulay and Dunn cups were all grist to his mill. Yet in all his distinguished career only one silver-mounted shinty came his way and that only as a result of special circumstances. The year he led Kyles to victory in the Celtic Cup was the one in which the practice of presenting a silver-mounted stick to the captain was discontinued.

However, such was the esteem in which this particular captain was held by no less a personage than one of his predecessors in the centre for Kyles – John Paterson – that he took it upon himself to obtain the necessary stick and present him with the missing honour.

When, in 1972, the time came for Alistair to stop playing, once again the decision was taken not by a Committee regretfully informing an old player that he was over the hill, but by the man himself. His decision was reached purely in what he considered to be the best interests of the team – a decision which illustrates perfectly the quality of the man who made it. For some years afterwards, Alistair dedicated himself to coaching the juniors so it was small wonder that the standards of shinty and conduct blossomed in Kyles shinty circles under his tutelage.

How then can we sum up the man who wore the Royal Blue with such distinction? First and foremost, he was a talented wielder of the caman – particularly renowned for the length and cleanness of his hitting allied to a natural ability to read the game. At no time in his long career did he ever fall foul of a referee nor yet of an opposing player. A credit to the jersey he wore. We mere mortals can claim with pride that, here at the Kyles, we have bred a man who has worthily earned the title "Prince of Shinty Players" – Alistair Arthur Chambers.

THE DISTRICT

We are now entering the Kyles of Bute, which many people regard as the most beautiful part of Scotland. For years guide-book writers have striven to capture the Kyles of Bute. Perhaps one of the best was a Victorian who wrote of the Kyles and the islands as "a necklace of shining waters studded with gems". Between the kirk and the ferry at Colintraive are the "Seven Sisters" – seven villas which were intended to start off Colintraive as a holiday resort. The name Colintraive is Gaelic and means "the swimming narrows", because the Highlanders swam their cattle across the strait at this point.

Now we reach the narrows and it is worth while to secure a good vantage point to see how little space the steamer has to get through. These are the Burnt Islands, named after a vitrified fort found there. On the right is Loch Riddon and ahead is Glen Caladh. The once proud castle here is now a ruin.

The steamer turns south here, leaving Loch Riddon behind us. Over on the Isle of Bute, to our left, are the "Maids of Bute" on the hillside. The Maids are a couple of boulders and they are painted in bright colours – red, black and white – to represent two old ladies in Welsh dress. Although this part of Bute is wild and uninhabited, the painting is still done. Nobody knows who started it, or why.

Now Tighnabruaich is in sight. This Gaelic name means "The house on the brae", and the house was an old inn. This is the end of the cruise and time is allowed on shore. There are tea-rooms, cafes and hotels in Tighnabruaich, and also places of refreshment at the two other holiday resorts served by this pier – Auchenlochan and Kames."

(Jack House, in *Sailing Down the Clyde*, CSPCo, 1965, price 6d. Breakfast was 6/6, Luncheon 9/-, and High Tea 7/6.)

131

"reality . . . is a team called Newtonmore"

Rivalry between the Kyles and the men of the North has been intense over the last century. In the interests of keen competition, we invited the notable Newtonmore former player, **John MacKenzie** to give a view from the opposition camp.

FIRST ENCOUNTER

John MacKenzie, Newtonmore

Being born into a family with great shinty traditions on both sides, from an early age I was to become acutely aware of the greatness of the club known to us all as Kyles Athletic. A team made up of men from that haven on the shores of the Kyles of Bute, and surrounding Tighnabruaich.

During my school days, I don't ever remember getting the opportunity to play against our counterparts from Kyles. However I was always reminded that until I did, I had not sampled the thrill of playing against the best. This was soon to become an ambition from those early days.

Having progressed through primary school years and on into secondary school with mates who went on to become legends in their own rights in the game, along with those older boys, I began to practise every night with our boyhood heroes – some of the greats of Newtonmore – John Paul MacKintosh. Johnny Campbell. Mike Aitken, Andrew Campbell, Gaby Fraser, Don Logan, Ewan McLaughlin and the Ralph brothers, George and Sandy – just a few of the legends of the game. They gave us the the experience and encouragement that was needed to spur us on, and to prepare us for what in future years was to be some of the greatest times of our, and particularly my own, shinty years.

At the age of fifteen, I remember being the youngest member of a Newtonmore second team which went on to secure a place in the Sutherland Cup final of 1961 against the great Kyles Athletic, albeit their second team, for the very first time.

Full of great expectations, I remember leaving home for Oban that late April morning, thinking what was ahead on that day, and what for me was the first encounter with Kyles Athletic.

On the bus down to Oban, chatting back and fore with the more experienced members of our team, I soon realised the importance of the occasion, and what it meant to them, and our supporters amongst whom were Alex Cattanach and Jimmy Sellar – both members of famous families who played for Newtonmore – when they gave their opinions on what was needed from our team to win the cup that day.

Arriving in Oban in torrential rain, we checked in to the Argyll Hotel which was to be our home for the next 24 hours and prepared for the game among our army of supporters – all offering their own comments on how to beat the Kyles, and hopefully take the cup home.

I realised just what really lay ahead in the game with names like Paterson, Nicolson, Turner, Jamieson, Crawford and so on being bandied about as opponents. It's little wonder that by this time I was very nervous and apprehensive about what I was about to experience. Nonetheless, encouraged by everyone, I took my place that day on Mossfield's rain-sodden surface and waited for the throw-up.

Soon I was to know what playing against the best was all about. Earlier that season we had won the junior league cup. we had reached the Strathdearn Cup final and here we were in the Sutherland Cup final. In the end we were soundly thrashed 6-1. From memory, I don't think the game itself was a classic, certainly not from Newtonmore's point of view. Nevertheless it was played with no quarter asked or given, and won on that occasion by the better team on the day. "Whaler" was my direct opponent, and dare I say it, I had to try very hard, and to grow up quickly to handle his experience.

Disappointed and sore, along with my team mates and supporters, I returned to the Argyll to discuss over and over again that night – and for days after – what went wrong and how we could turn things round in the future to beat the boys from Kyles.

Between the years of 1959 and 1963, major rebuilding of Newtonmore's first team was taking place and many great names began to step down quietly. I recall an invitation being extended to

Newtonmore to visit Tighnabruaich to open the new playing field and provide the opposition to Kyles for a game to commemorate the occasion. this was to set the scene for a new era for both clubs and some memorable times between Kyles and Newtonmore.

Trying to establish myself along with other new faces in the Newtonmore first team from 1962 onwards, I can vividly remember the occasion of my first winner's medal in the Torlundy Cup final at King George V Park in Fort William. This, however, was against Oban Camanachd and not the great Kyles Athletic, who earlier that year had beaten Kilmallie in the Camanachd Cup final. For the next three of four years the new names in the Newtonmore team began to establish themselves and together we began to challenge again for the major honours. Another invitation was extended to the Newtonmore Club to play Kyles at Tighnabruaich for the Deer-Stalker shield and this was, finally, to be my invitation into playing against the best.

I recall that September day on the rain sodden field, the inexperience of the new look Newtonmore against the much fancied home team, and athough beaten "again", a great game was enjoyed by all the players on both sides. The score was 6-2 or 6-3.

The after match occasion in the Kames Hotel set the foundations for lifelong friendships between myself – and I know my fellow team-mates – and lads such as Will MacRae, Barnie Crawford, Wee Tom Nick, Neil Blair, the Jamieson brothers – Chick and Jim – the Turner brothers and so on, all being part of that memorable event. One person, however, who stood out as the host for that weekend was the great Captain MacRae of Ballimore. He, along with that other great exponent and bard, Celly Paterson, made the occasion one never to be forgotten.

I got home that weekend late on Sunday night. But there were others I know who didn't reach home until at least the next Tuesday! (Incidentally, my next visit to the Kames Hotel after that occasion – and I have been to Tighnabruaich many times since – was in 1994 when Newtonmore were regrettably knocked out of the Scottish Cup by the home team. I wasn't playing but the friendships were still there and as strong as ever.)

Onward then from this occasion to our next game against one another and this was to be the 1966 Scottish Cup final – and what a struggle that was to be!

Knowing what to expect, the Newtonmore team under Jimmy Gaul, who was the trainer then, were considered never to be fitter. Better prepared than ever they took the field that day at the Bught Park with great expectations. Alas by the end of the hour and a half, having scored first, missed two penalties and with Kyles' Bobby Nicolson absolutely outstanding in goal, we ended up on the wrong side of a 3-2 score line. What did we have to do to beat the Kyles? That question was asked over and over again until the next opportunity which was to be some four years later.

In between 1966 and 1970 the Newtonmore team began to establish a consistency about it. with names like Chisholm, Cheyne, MacGregor, Kirk, Ritchie, Smith, Sellar, Campbell, Stewart, Fraser, Ralph, MacKenzie and so on and eventually with great ambition and commitment, in 1970 we went on to meet Kyles in the Scottish final on the Dell, Kingussie.

This, for Newtonmore, and for me, was to be one of the most memorable games ever in a blue and white strip. And against the great Kyles of Bute. A goal down to Kyles in two or three minutes scored by Neil Blair, I thought, "Here we go, not again."

Not this time, though, with the huge home support and the wonderful team spirit. We eventually began to play to our capabilities and by half-time we were 5-1 up. That day the team went on to win 7-1 with some outstanding performances, particulary by Brian Stewart, Johnny Campbell, John Fraser, and Sandy Ralph – the four forwards for Newtonmore on that occasion.

With great sportsmanship, I recall both teams at the end embracing one another and saying 'well done' or 'hard luck' as the case may have been – and for the Newtonmore boys the elation at having at last beaten the great Kyles after almost ten years.

That weekend and for days later was a time of great celebration and enjoyment for the boys and everybody in the village of Newtonmore and this included the Kyles boys who on their way home on the Sunday stopped off at the "Balavil" and like the sportsmen they were, joined in as though they themselves had won the cup.

1971 saw again the two teams meet in the final on the Bught, with the score ending the same, thus signalling the new Newtonmore era was perhaps in being.

The next two or three years saw both teams avoid each other in the Scottish Cup final, but the were to play in the MacAulay final once or twice with honours shared and pick up the big on once each, before meeting again on the Dell in the 1975 final.

Another epic occasion ending in a 3-3 draw with Newtonmore at one time 3-0 up and Kyles fighting back in the second half for the deserved draw. Chick Turner and Ginger MacNeill, who won the Albert Smith Memorial that day, were an inspiration to all around them.

The replay at Fort William the following week was another close encounter played in great conditions and brilliant sunshine. It ended in a 1-0 win for Newtonmore – how much closer can you get?

The 1976 season saw both teams again contest the Scottish Cup final, this time at the Bught Park. Conditions underfoot were at their usual best at this venue but overhead the weather was somewhat unpleasant with almost constant rain throughout the game

This was no excuse as it was the same for both sides and Kyles were to be the masters on that day. It was obvious from the start that they meant business and were determined to ensure "the big one" went south to Argyll on the following Sunday.

Tom Nicolson, who incidentally was usually my direct opponent and director in chief of the Kyles, had a blinder that day. Chick Jamieson in defence and Barnie in the middle were both in top form and with their dominance and leadership they made life very difficult for Newtonmore. In the end Kyles all round ability gave them the well deserved victory on the day.

So, ten years had passed by this time, from that first cup final in Inverness and both teams had shared the same amount of wins in the Scottish.

The MacAulay Cup final of 1976 the following week in Oban saw Newtonmore get some revenge over Kyles when they went on to win by a 6-0 margin. Good, but not the same as the "big one".

The years of 1977-78 and 1979-80 saw the same two teams contest the Scottish final with Newtonmore winning three out of the four matches, with 1980 being the last time the teams were to meet in the final. all of these finals were closely contested games with one or two goals at the most separating the teams.

Major restructuring of the Camanachd Association came in 1983 when the open draw was introduced to the Scottish Cup and significantly it brought together for the first time in the final two south teams – Kyles and Strachur. Watching this game from the sidelines was a new experience. In the end, a closely contested match was won on the day by the more experienced Kyles team.

Both Kyles and Newtonmore have gone on to win the "big one" against other prominent opposition, but not since that day in 1980 on the Dell have they played against one another in the Scottish Cup final.

1983 saw the end of my personal shinty-playing career. Injuries and work commitments saw me play my last game against the great Kyles on the Eilan. The game marked the opening of the refurbished pitch and I recall with pride marching on to the field behind two of the game's great stalwarts – Celly Paterson and Jock Paul MacKintosh, our respective club Presidents/Chieftains. This was an honour in itself of the highest degree.

Time does not stand still and as it progressed both clubs were to lose their two great ambassadors in the game. Firstly Celly, then Jock. I remember with much sadness but also with great pride their funerals.

The attendance at both indicated the respect each had commanded in the game and had the whole world of shinty reminiscing on their life and times in the game they loved so much.

The standing both Kyles and Newtonmore have had in the game was recognised by the Camanachd Association when they were asked to compete against each other home and away for the Association Centenary Year 1993 Challenge Trophy. For me, these were both memorable events with representation from a wide area in the game – and lengthy discussion and crack on the past and future in which both clubs I hope still want, and need, to be part of.

These are just some of the great times I enjoyed in shinty. In conclusion, my life associated with, and the enjoyment of playing the game in particular, was enhanced by the friendships made with Kyles. Since stopping playing I have had opportunities to continue the bond through playing, or maybe trying to play as a veteran, both at home and in Tighnabruaich

The wonderful experiences and the continuance of the friendships is firmly cemented by the respect which over the years has been of the highest for that Great Team – the Kyles Athletic Shinty Club.

May you have the very best of luck in your next hundred years.

Jim Jamieson lifts the cup in 1965

Kyles Athletic Camanachd Cup Winners 1968
Donald Shaw, captain

THE SIXTIES

When Kyles won the Sutherland Cup in 1961, in the game so graphically described by John MacKenzie, the club ushered in a decade of success that stands comparison with the twenties. Which was the greater depends on the age of the person making the impossible judgement. The records are contained in this book and the balance seems to come out pretty evenly.

When the seniors recaptured the Camanachd Cup in 1962, and Alistair Macrae emulated his father's feat of the twenties, they started a run which was to bring four more victories in the major competition, and between 1960 and 1970 (inclusive) they took the Celtic Cup six times and the MacAulay five. In 1966 they completed the 'grand slam' in an unbeaten competition run that was to be halted by ancient rivals Inveraray in the Camanachd semifinal.

The playing field seemed to be an important factor in this success. Odd as it may seem now, it was a 'state of the art' pitch when it opened. 'Graham's boys' relished a surface on which the ball would run rather than plug. And they learned not only to cope with the slope but to use it – an art which some of the better visiting players quickly mastered too. Some of the best games were the late summer friendlies – and the North–South Argyll clashes for the Deerstalker Shield. These brought great players from Oban, like Donnie MacCallum, and Lochfyneside, like Donnie Campbell in tussles that succeeded in being both exhibition matches and highly competitive cup-ties.

It was in the 1960s that John MacKellar's 'Tighnabruaich ball' came into its own. Its clear superiority over anything else on the market became quickly apparent to any club encountering Kyles and orders started to flow in.

The alternatives, by comparison, were reminiscent of the wooden balls of the days before the great Sandy MacKellar of Cowal. John learned the craft of ball-making, and shoe-making, from his uncle – who stuck to his bootmaker's last in the shop next to Smith's village boatshed until well into his nineties.

John's premises were at the other end of the village, beside the burn, and though far from glamorous housed the lasts of many famous feet. His main income came from hand producing made-to-measure footwear for the rich and famous.

Shoe repairs and shinty ball-making were sidelines that verged on the charitable.

John MacKellar, maker of the Tighnabruaich ball, has a visitor to his workshop

The triumphant 1976 team – sweeping all before them
Back – Maitland Black, Duncan MacNeill, Tom Nicolson, Ronald Irvine,
Peter Turner, Iain MacBride, Russell Thorburn, Charles Turner

Front – Neil Black, Billy Paterson, Charles Jamieson, George Nicolson, Scott Turner, Neil Blair, John Paterson

The 1974 cup winning team –
captain Russell Thorburn, man of the match Tom Nicolson

THE SEVENTIES

Douglas Lowe

The memory plays tricks, but my recollection of the Kyles team of the seventies is that they were heroes all, overturning huge deficits as underdogs against Newtonmore in that epic series of six Camanachd finals in a row, real Roy of the Rovers stuff.

None more so than that Neil Blair winner at Kingussie for a 6–5 success in the last of that same-again sequence which wasn't in the seventies at all but in 1980. Still, we won't let a mere fact get in the way of counting that one as part of the seventies as well. It was certainly the same era and the last great one which will live in the minds of all who witnessed it.

The memory, however, does not tally with the records. Between 1970 and 1980 Kyles and Newtonmore met in the final eight times and Kyles won only twice. The first two in 1970 and 1971 were 7–1 reversals which can be glossed over happily here because the writer saw neither and they were really from a different era.

In that decade Kyles did win a third in 1974, but that was against Kingussie. Perhaps the reason Kyles seemed to have done better was the 1975 final at Kingussie when the boys in blue fought back from 3–0 down to 3–3 – then lost the replay 1–0 at Fort William. That has to go down as a defeat even if it seemed like a moral victory at the time.

The underdog status was hotly disputed also, with Celly Paterson and his Newtonmore counterpart, Jock Paul MacKintosh, each going to pains beforehand to put up a smokescreen claim that the other was more likely to win. You tended to suspect, though, that in the minds of the sometimes arrogant north, Newtonmore were always expected to win.

Another reason that Kyles team are remembered as fine fellows well met was my first encounter with them in the Spring of 1974.

As a member of the worst shinty team of that era, St Andrews University, we had arrived at Tighnabruaich for an overnight stay with our tails between our legs following a 16–0 defeat by Strachur in the second round of the Camanachd Cup (we had a bye in the first round, in case you were wondering).

On then to Kames Hotel to sample the local nightlife. Richard McKinlay – who went on to found the now defunct Livingston Shinty Club – and I encountered the larger-than-life Jock Turner with whom we were acquainted through our regular thrashings by the then Glasgow Police.

As the night developed we met the Kyles team one by one and sometimes six by six, and arranged with Scott Turner and John Drum a friendly for the following day. It was to be Kyles v St Andrews in the first half, and then the teams were to be mixed up to make a game of it. On the Sabbath in this Free Presbyterian stronghold? Heaven forbid! But the committee were consulted and a blind eye was to be turned.

It remains one of my great regrets that this game never took place. The predominantly English faction in our team didn't fancy another hiding. Suffice to say that the atmosphere in the team bus on the journey back east was not good. Still, we had been welcomed magnificently into the brotherhood of shinty, and the friendships have lasted, continuing a family link started by my father, who did the BBC radio commentaries on the shinty finals at that time.

We heard later that Kyles soon afterwards had given Strachur a thorough turning over and had told them, "That was for what you did to St Andrews." Well, isn't it nice to have a big brother to look after you.

It is hard to do justice to the Kyles team of the seventies in an article of this length, and the best I can think of is to check through the records of that six-in-a-row series and pick the Kyles and Newtonmore teams on the basis of most appearances. It works out:

Kyles Athletic: Billy Paterson, Chic Jamieson, George Nicolson, Neil Blair, Scott Turner, Iain MacBride, Kerr Crawford, Peter Turner, Chic Turner, Tommy Nicolson, Robert Baxter, Russell Thorburn. Substitutes – Duncan MacNeill, Ronnie Irvine, Colin MacColl.

Newtonmore: Hugh Chisholm, David Cheyne, Donald MacGregor, John MacKenzie, Sandy Ralph, Angus MacRae, Ken Smith, David Ritchie, John Fraser, Ken MacKintosh, Iain Bain, George Fraser. Substitutes – Brian Stewart, Jim MacBean.

Curiously, these two precise teams never actually met, but this was the Kyles XII that played in 1976 at Inverness and won 4–2, and it was the Newtonmore XII that played in 1977 and 1978 winning 5–3 and 3–2 at Glasgow and Fort William respectively.

That would tend to suggest that the sides were so well matched that what mattered on the day was whether the strongest possible side could be fielded. As keen as the rivalry was the friendship and mutual respect that developed which, in a sense, is far more important than the results themselves.

As editor of the *Shinty Yearbook* at the time I would write leaders suggesting it was a bad thing that the same two teams were meeting in the showpiece every year. In a way perhaps it was, but in hindsight the finals since have only on a few occasions matched the same atmosphere, crowds of 6000-plus, and sheer excitement. It was an era to savour.

Through thick and thin, Tighnabruaich and Kames have always been hospitable and friendly places to the visitor, especially to those on shinty business. No doubt there always will be a keen sense of anticipation by those who journey down the winding Cowal road.

(Douglas Lowe is a sports journalist with *The Herald*.)

Kerr 'Barney' Crawford is cheered on to the pitch

BARNEY

Ronald Martin

Over the years many great players have worn the famous Royal Blue jersey of Kyles Athletic. One of those is a man whose record as a player speaks for itself. Nineteen South Division One Championships, one National League title, five MacAulay Cup, twelve Celtic and an incredible eight Camanachd Cup winners medals is a haul that most players can only dream about, but the Kerr 'Barney' Crawford it is a reality.

Barney played his first senior match at the tender age of seventeen but surprisingly not for the Kyles. His first match was in 1959 for Glasgow Mid-Argyll and the opponents that day were Glasgow Inverness. He continued to turnout for Mid-Argyll whilst at Agricultural College, but was soon to establish himself in the Kyles team when he cam home after finishing his studies.

Over the next thirty years he was to establish himslef as one of the best known and most respected men in shinty. But what was his most memorable moment?

"I had lots over the years, but probably being captain of the winning Scottish Cup team in 1969 is the one that stands out."

Barney won another seven in the years before and after that memorable moment when he held aloft the Camanachd Cup. Along the way he watched many players come and go, but which players did he admire when he was younger?

"Lots. But I think that Ian Irvine was the best players I have ever seen."

Great praise from one of the greats himself, but Barney has praise for another man whom he obviously holds in great respect. Of all the characters of his playing days there is one he remembers above the rest.

"Celly. Over the years he was always there through thick and thin. Always a character. I even wrote a song about one of his antics."

But now with a cabinet full of memories, Barney is looking forward to his future with Kyles. His dedication is still evident, as he now spends his spare time with the young stars of the future at Tighnabruaich Primary School. His enthusiasm for the game is undimmed, and typified in his answer when I asked him what his hopes for the future were.

"I hope to keep enough of the youngsters interested in playing shinty and to ensure that there will always be a good pool of players available."

Let's hope that some of his character rubs off on the kids because if it does then Kyles have a bright and successful future ahead of them.

But what for Kyles future? How does Barney see the next hundred years going for Kyles?

"Who knows what it will be like in another hundred years. Maybe the matches will be played on computer. But really, the future of the club is up to the players. They are the ones who must commit themselves both on and off the field if they want the club to continue and to be as successful as it has been in the past. If they are prepared to be as dedicated as the players of the last one years, then I have no doubt that there will still be a Kyles team in a hundred years' time, still winning their fair share of the silverware."

The late Celly Paterson was a player whose character stands fondly in the memory of Kerr 'Barney' Crawford (opposite). Celly died in 1986. "Shinty is the poorer for his passing," wrote GY Slater

Kyles Glendaruel captain Duncan MacVicar is held aloft with the Camanachd Cup in 1983

THE COL-GLEN CONNECTION

Alex McNaughton

The East Kyle and the West Kyle make up the famous Kyles of Bute. On the West Kyle is the heart and home of the equally famous Kyles Athletic, Tighnabruaich.

On the East Kyle, and just round the corner, lies Tighnabruaich's near neighbour, Colintraive. A few miles further North is the community of Glendaruel. Colintraive and Glendaruel – later known as Col-Glen – also form a proud shinty community, though never having aspired to the great achievements of Kyles.

Prior to improvements in roads and transport, Tighnabruaich was much more accessible by sea, which is possibly partly why in the early thirties two players moved from Col-Glen to play senior with the Kyles, thus setting up a connection that still exists to this day.

John MacVicar, Glendaruel, and Hamish McIntyre, Colintraive, were the first players from Col-Glen to move and play for Kyles. These two were closely followed by Archie Carmichael, Hamish's brother Duncan (better known as Bunty) and Walter Robertson.

Kyles were involved in four Scottish Cup finals in the 1930s, winning in 1935 against the great North team of the time, Caberfeidh, by 6-4 in Inverness. John MacVicar, Hamish McIntyre and Archie Carmichael were all involved in that final. In fact Hamish McIntyre, though not captain that year, actually captained the team that day.

Over the years since the Second World War, players have continued to travel from Colintraive and Glendaruel to play for Kyles. Duncan MacVicar, John's brother, also appeared in a Kyles jersey.

Also related is Duncan MacVicar, of the next generation. His brother Ronald, Donald MacPhail, and Kenneth Allan are all involved in the modern-day Kyles, proving things don't change much – there are still MacVicars from Glendaruel playing in Kyles.

Over the years changes in the format of the leagues, together with cup games have brought many encounters between Col-Glen and Kyles Juniors, and although there was always intense rivalry on the field there was also a camaraderie and respect among the players which has kept the Kyles–Col-Glen connection alive.

It is a great achievement to celebrate a centenary, and your near neighbours in Colintraive and Glendaruel say, "Well done, Kyles Athletic."

Alex McNaughton has been a referee and Camanachd Association member for many years.

Four Col-Glen men in Kyles team in 1939

MUNRO CAMANS

Patricia Shaw

It did not take long to find Willie Munro. While there are no fewer than sixteen Munro(e)s in the local telephone directory, there could only be one who lives at Caman Cottage. And when I asked about the correct spelling of his name I was told in no uncertain terms that an added 'e' is the English version – and what would an Englishman know of the making of camans?

Originally from Inveraray, and a renowned family of boat-builders – Donald Munro, 1812, lately of Kilmun – came a family of sons whose skills have been involved in building some of the finest ships of the Clyde.

And so it was a natural transition in later years to use these skills and experience, a love of wood combined with a love of the sport, to start a post-retirement hobby-come-business making what what was to become the forerunner of today's camans.

Willie Munro was the inspiration behind Munro Camans. He could remember his father using steam to bend hickory sticks before the last war. And Willie has that rare gift of being able to visualise a process in his head and then follow it through with the practical application.

In 1974, he made inquiries about the supply of hickory, visited a big yard in England and there and then bought "all that was lying around on the floor".

And so was born the first-ever full-length laminated shinty stick.

The blocks of hickory were cut into lengths with a tipped saw. This gave a fine, smooth surface on either side, without the need for planing. The laminate could then be glued, pressed together, bent into shape, and dried. The 'block' was then ready to be cut into individual sticks, narrowed and angled to suit the position of play, or the individual player.

Willie's late brother, Donald, who managed a boatyard in Windermere, was able to supply all the necessary information relating to the strength ond properties of the glueing process. And just to keep it in the family came retired boatbuilder brother Calum, to lend a hand. Calum had played for Kilmun and for North Bute, two junior teams of the thirties.

But the business side of Munro Camans was incidental. Come Saturdays and the brothers would be on the sidelines, themselves a fixture, supporting Kyles with a passion that is second to none. For these fine old gentlemen, the satisfaction came from being part of the spirit of the game itself, and from the camaderie they found within every club.

And that is the essence of the game.

Trish Shaw is the daughter of Pat Currie and wife of Donald Shaw – both Camanachd winning captains.

158

Neil Blair busy making camans in his Kames workshop

NEIL BLAIR started making camans for Kyles while still a player in the early 1970s. He had at that time just set up in business with team-mate Robert Baxter after the demise of the ill-fated Portavadie project.

"I went to see Willie Munro," says Neil, "and he was very helpful. But he didn't tell me how to make sticks."

According to Neil Blair, making sticks – and he now

159

provides several hundreds every year for teams throughout Scotland – is something you learn yourself. And have to re-learn almost year by year, such are the changes in the game! At the time of the visit to his Kames workshop, he was preparing a batch of sticks for Skye, who wanted an extra lamina.

"The game has changed a lot even since I was playing," says Neil. "It is played much more in the ground now. You have to make the kinds of sticks the players want – and I have to take note of that. I also make sure that when I get a complaint, I do something about it." So while the sticks are offered basically in the three traditional forms – back, midfield and forward – a lot of players prefer camans designed for positions other than their own.

His workshop contains some impressive machinery – purchased originally with the help of a small grant from the then Highland Board – but much more impressive is the eye he brings to the job. He is constantly squinting along the cas of a caman to ensure it is straight, and hefting it to gauge the 'feel' and balance of the product.

His partnership with his old Kyles buddy Robert Baxter has now dissolved and the shinty-making has expanded considerably. But it remains to a great degree a labour of love. Having started on the basis of making a contribution to the club that had given him so much as a player, he moved on through his stick making to make a contribution to the game as a whole.

The hourly rate is niggardly compared to that of his building and joinery work – and prices are kept down on the delivery side by the elaborate lengths he goes to to make sure sticks are carriage-free. Whether to Kyles of Caberfeidh, through a network of transport contacts, lifts or personally, orders are delivered at no extra cost.

But making camans offers a unique competitive satisfaction. "Every time I make sticks for Newtonmore, I think to myself, I'm still beating them at their own game!"

POSTSCRIPT FROM ARCADIA

A Allan Neill

I had a premonition. It came like a cold wind. A messenger arrived to uplift the Camanachd Cup and when it was removed from the perch atop the Victorian gantry in the public bar, it was handed to me to be carried to the waiting courier. That's when it happened. It was the weirdest thing, but the instant the Cup passed from my possession I was overwhelmed by a certainty that never would I be made responsible for its safekeeping again.

The sensation passed quickly, but the echo of the foreboding remained. I thought I had become inured to the frequent comings and goings of the trophy. It had been removed many times before. Sometimes for inscribing. Sometimes it would disappear for a season or two when, by some mischance, an upstart team laid temporary claim to its ownership. But it always came back. After all, the Camanachd Cup's return is woven into the history of the village.

It was almost sacrilegious to believe that its departure was permanent. Had not local rituals evolved to accompany its re-emergence? First its silver grandeur is trawled round the homes and watering-holes of the village. During this noisy meandering a flow of liquid to shame the Niagara pours from its cornucopic interior. Everyone is seen to be given the opportunity to pay tribute. Then, it disappears into the hinterland of the the farming community. What mysterious rituals are enacted when removed from public view are only for those who take part in the rites, but they can be guessed at if the overdrive gear of the imagination is engaged.

Thereafter, almost ectoplasmically, it manifests itself in

161

"To an Eastcoaster's eye the contest resembled . . . a kind of rugby with weapons."

Jamieson's bakehouse shop window in the centre of the village. There it stands majestically be-ribboned and boastfully presented, trumpeting its importance to tourist and local alike, and there it remains until its high profile stretches communal contentment to exhaustion.

It is dispatched then, and only then, to its caretakers – the public bar staff of the Royal Hotel. That is the routine, the acknowledged ritual. It had been happening for a hundred yeas. Why should it stop now?

Despite this thought my premonition persisted. Was it not irrational for me to be haunted by such a concern. After all, I had never been a shinty player, and I must confess there was a time when I looked upon the sport with a degree of disapproval. When first I witnessed a shinty match doubts were secretly harboured whether the playing of the game should be allowed. To an Eastcoaster's eye the contest resembled, as near as dammit, armed conflict. A kind of rugby with weapons. A form of frank vandalism. In short, war was waged. Perhaps my background made it impossible for me to appreciate the finer points of the mayhem?

Today a Highland village can appear as Scottish as sugared porridge, but in the fifties, when lawyers were trusted and bankers had not yet succumbed to criminality, the ambience was as Celtic as a ceilidh. As a newly-arrived twenty-five year old brought up to the rhythms of a city I had many cultural subtleties to absorb before I could interpret anything of what was going on correctly. I concluded, therefore, that while I considered shinty to be barbaric, nevertheless, the skills required to survive its rigours were masterly, and by that token, and only when I was prepared to stretch the meaning of the word 'game' to farcical limits, was I able to understand how such a wielding of camans might be believed to be a sport. Pompous twit

162

that I was. I couldn't see what I was looking at.

I first glimpsed the Camanachd Cup at Ballimore almost four decades ago. At the time it made little impression. In fact I saw two of shinty's premier trophies simultaneously. The other was the Celtic Cup and my attention was drawn to it rather than to its grander companion.

The smaller prize is a simple goblet but of such perfect shape that its appeal is truly seductive. A Sophia Loren in silver. My attention was further distracted by an unlikely object welded to the wall of the room. It was a propellor. No doubt a varnished relic of some past glory. At the time this unexpected decoration stirred my imagination much more than the silverware on display. This bizarre memento was the keepsake of Captain Duncan MacRae, the Laird of Ballimore.

In truth he was more than a mere Laird. He was MacRae of MacRae of Eilean Donan, a genuine example of a species now almost extinct – a Highland Chief. Everything about him radiated this truth. As well as height he had the girth of a colossus. His upper body bulk was supported by tree-trunk legs easily made visible by a kilt cut to unfashionable length. On ordinary days he looked impressive, on High days and Holyrood days he was unbelievable. Wrapped in his Highland plaid, buckled and belted, dirked and glengarryed he evoked a wonder which bedazzled the senses. A portrait gallery phantom come to life to stir the dormant tribal memory. He looked magnificent.

Initially, because of my city rearing, I found it difficult to regard him as anything other than good theatre. His community significance had long been neutered. Politically he was a living anachronism. A social dinosaur. Time had moved on and a climate change had left him stranded. However, this truth was avoided, and to have articulated the thought would have been considered traitorous. The

163

"shinty was . . . broadsword practice perfected"

Highland chieftain still inhabits a place in the hearts and minds of Highland populations and like MacRae many of them were, and are, distinctive and extraordinary men.

One such was Lord Lovat who died recently. Lovat was a Second World War hero with a matchless record for courage and daring.

It was he who led his men into battle from the front with his personal piper playing within earshot. It tugs one's heart that he is gone. We are all diminished by his passing and left poignantly musing if ever we will see his like again.

MacRae and Lovat were men of the same ilk. Fashioned from the rock of our country.

Once when captured in battle MacRae was put to torture for displaying unacceptable defiance in the presence of his captors. The indignity of that experience was never to be erased from his psyche, nor were the marks of the wounds inflicted upon his body. No man can suffer such extremes of brutality and survive undamaged. The Turks, whom he had offended by his bearing, suspended him from a tree to be lashed into a humbler mien. They failed, of course. His demeanour was ingrained. The outrage of the ordeal was remembered by MacRae not for the pain but for the dishonour it reflected upon all who were involved. The barbarity displayed by his captors placed them beneath consideration. They were men beyond the pale, Visigoths, and were to be defied to the crack of doom with a show of valour to match the vigour of the contempt.

In his later years MacRae developed two abiding passions. Whisky and shinty. Both are inebriating, both are addictive. Through a devotional relationship he had come to understand the pure nature of both. Whisky made bearable the dark angers that lurked in his centre, and shinty was a symphony of physicality which suffused his spirit with pleasure. A sport with purpose. Activity sprung from

164

atavistic memory. Agility transmogrified to artform. It was broadsword practice perfected. The skills of the game are ingrained in the blood of the Highlander by the historic shedding of ancestral blood upon ancient battlefields.

Yes, he knew the twin fires which warmed his marrow and took his comfort from both. Never a man to stint on his pleasures he lavished a generous proportion of his wealth to pursue a harmonious mingling of the two enthusiasms. Kyles Athletic committee meetings were often Bacchanalian as a result. When the Captain appeared, or 'Yuk-Yuk' as he was nicknamed after his manner of laughing, those present would smile at the knowledge that a good night was about to unravel.

MacRae was a marvellous motivator. By timely interruptions he never failed to relax meetings into a state of noisy confidence, and unheard-of unanimity. Shining faces wearing broad smiles would announce inspired team selections with gleeful panache. Halcyon years were enjoyed by Kyles Athletic and the whisky bill was obscene.

The team was 'Yuk-Yuk's obsession. They were his boys. His trusted troops. The deliverers of the 'blue riband'. Skill and purpose brought awards, but when combined with sporting elegance and flair, the trophy was the bounty of dreamers – the Scottish Camanachd Cup – the Holy Grail. MacRae and the committee expected nothing less and for many years Silvo was constantly on invoice.

My cynicism about the game evaporated over the years. In the end I was a convert. My 'Road to Damascus' experience happened when I saw Alistair Chambers play. I was transfixed by his easy grace and co-ordination in the midst of tumult. He was phenomenal. To remember one man when such a galaxy of talent was involved is inexcusable but his gentlemanly disposition left him with no equal in my memory.

If other 'Gentlemen of the Year' awards are to be bestowed then the list would be long. Old Jimmy Nicolson comes easily to mind together with his fellow enthusiasts of the MacRae era, Celly Paterson, Neil Drum, Dan MacRae and Neil Nicolson. When these men held sway the club prospered mightily.

Although there was never a paucity of praiseworthy players to pick from, the elusive trick was to weld an invincible unit from the reservoir of talent. This was achieved by collective osmosis made possible by social bonding. Talking men simply sitting at a table in the corner of the bar would hatch conspiracies to shape sporting exhibitions of electrifying spectacle.

The corner table in the bar has long been abandoned. The shinty committees congregate elsewhere to conspire these days, and the new afficionados wrestle with complexities unimagined by their forebears. Thirty years have wrought economic and cultural change to complicate their task.

Within that short span a new road has carved the end of comfortable isolation. A tourist pattern established for over a century has been blown apart by the attractions of foreign travel. The volcanic eruption of Portavadie mutated the village from order into black gold-rush carnage, and when this debacle was abandoned it left an uncompensated-for nightmare still to be properly awakened from.

A further flurry of body-blows was waiting to fall. Two recessions sandwiching an inflation, Chernobyl, a currency implosion, a property collapse – it all seemed as if the punishments were biblical rather than political.

As the population groggily struggles from the canvas, bleary vision reveals that a new environment has evolved and a new morality has been born. The old mood of community enterprise has been diminished and something akin to a suburb of Glasgow mentality has formed. It is too early to assess whether these convulsions will eventually prove to be beneficial. For the moment it is enough to have survived it all.

But what now for the champions of Scotland's 1500-year-old game? In the emerging brave new world can a village of six hundred souls struggling with the disciplines of basic survival continue to sustain the will and energy required to field a champion team? Doubts were frankly expressed in no less a publication than the *Sunday Times* of 2nd April 1995. The correspondent Adam Jones feared that Kyles Athletic players are so encumbered with family and employment worries that enthusiasm for shinty might not escape impairment.

He should have no fears on that account. The community may be brought low but dedication to the sport will never be dimmed or diminished by hardship. On the contrary. The shinty playing families of Irvine, Turner, Blair, Mobeck, Taylor, et al, understand, unlike Mr Jones, that it was the determination to triumph over affliction which inspired the birth of the sport. In times of hardship a purer type of shinty is played. The irritant ingredient stiffens the resolve. Shinty is brought back to its roots. No, apprehensions for the game lie elsewhere.

Shinty as a spectacle is attracting an expanding interest. Media and commercial attention lurks in the wings and threatens to catapult the sport into new dimensions of popularity. And then what? Camanachd Association (2000) plc, perhaps?

Unless wise heads prevail, a transformation could engulf the game with regrettable results. Quicksands are everywhere to lure the easily enticed or naive. Kyles Athletic should be wary not to bargain their proud heritage for a mess of potage. As champions they have responsibility to the ancient traditions of the game and the purity of its spectacle.

Soon Joe Donachie's amusing mural proclaiming Kyles Athletic 'roolers' of the sport is due to be obliterated from the wall of the public bar of the Royal Hotel. Will there be another created in the future? Without doubt.

In the end, logical analysis dispels all uncertainty. A valorous history in the sport will see to it. Class counts. The local soil is impregnated with inspiration and from it will be reaped the harvest of our future sporting success.

And remember this: a fallen Arcadia is Arcadia still.

Allan Neill is proprietor of the Royal Hotel, which has a long association with Kyles Athletic.

SCHOOLS

(from *Shinty! 100 Years of the Camanachd Association* by Hugh Dan MacLennan)

The Schools' Camanachd Association was formed in 1937, and its founders were, interestingly, connected with two of the game's strongholds. Ewen A. MacQueen, a teacher of technical subjects, and his brother Dr Malcolm C. MacQueen had spent their formative years in the Kyles of Bute. Being interested in all manner of outdoor activities, they had formed a close connection with the Kyles club and when they moved north to Inverness, they quickly took up the game among kindred spirits.

It became apparent to Ewen MacQueen, who had returned to the town after a period working in Yorkshire, that there was a pressing need for some organised form of the game in Highland schools, and by 1937 he had almost single-handedly planned the formation of the new Association. In the first two years, with the whole-hearted support of the local authorities, interest spread rapidly from the Isle of Skye to Argyll, and ultimately as far south as Glasgow. At the outset, the handsome John MacPherson trophy was put up for annual competition, with teams participating on a league basis. Kingussie High were the first winners in 1938, followed in 1939 by Oban High.

The MacPherson, for which Tighnabruaich School competed in the post-war era, was at that time for pupils below the statutory leaving age of fifteen, i.e. in Third Year or under. Six-year schools could include pupils who, while they were in Fourth Year, were not yet old enough to leave school – whether or not they intended to stay on. The MacPherson Cup is now for pupils aged under 14 at 1st August in the session beginning that month – ie for First and Second Year pupils; the Wade Cup is for under 16s on the same basis,and the MacBean Cup is for senior pupils. There are two primary competitions – the MacKay Cup and the Bank of Scotland Cup.

Six-a-sides games for younger players are now well established
The above team of Kyles lads picked up a trophy at Taynuilt in June 1982
back – Robert Baxter, Ewan McDonald and Norman McDonald
front – Douglas Shaw, Alistair Wren, Fraser McDonald and David Taylor

Another trophy winning Kyles sixes team – winners of the Aviemore Cup 3–2 against Kingussie in 1985
(back) Jamie Strickland, John Blair, Iain Taylor, Iain Fletcher
(front) Craig Blair, Ewan Callan, Kevin McKay, Sandy Jamieson

SHINTY

(as seen from the primary school)

Our first time to a shinty match was a disaster. We all went
to Strachur on a very hot day. As we got out of the car my
brother got bitten by a dog. We went to the first aid tent and
just as we were going in a shinty ball was flying through
the air and hit my mum on the face. We thought mum
would end up in hospital but the kind nurse kept putting
ice on her face. Poor mum had a swollen face for the rest of
our holidays. And I didn't think she would like to go to a
Shinty match again.

Vicky

I've got a video of Dad winning the Camanachd Cup. He
was very happy. Dad doesn't like whisky but he drank
some out of the cup.

Amanda, 7

My dad won 50 medals for shinty. I played in the Jamieson
Cup – our team won. I like to play forward.

Grant, 7

Not Fair! Go Away!

I go to all the shinty practices but I'm never allowed to play
in the games, but when there isn't enough people to make a
team they come to me saying "Oh, we don't have enough to
make a team, can you play?"

And I always say, "No! Go away!" Because I don't think
it's fair! And they use me as a last resource.

Clare, 11

10 Minutes To Go

It's just 10 minutes to go lads and ladies
Put on your helmets
Put on your strips
And the best of luck
And for goodness sake don't fall in the muck
Put in your block
Don't flock together
Stay on your man or woman
Stick in there and don't take forever to get the ball
Oh and I need someone tall for the throw up.

Gareth, 10

I like to go to games. I like to see Kyles play against Oban
Camanachd because they are both good teams and it's a
good game. My dad is the best 'goalie' and Peter Mobeck
plays well. Skin and Dan are good too.

Roddy, 7

I like to see them taking shy's. Tom Whyte is really good at
it.

Andrew, 7

I got a drink out of the big cup and David Taylor had it on
his head.

Lorna, 4

When I was watching shinty the ball went in the muck field
and I went for it. I fell in the muck. It was at Glenurquhart.

Angus, 7

"Representatives from the local shinty team provide weekly coaching sessions which are very popular with senior pupils," said inspectors from Strathclyde Region's Quality Assurance Unit approvingly when they visited Tighnabruaich Primary School in August 1994.

But a year later, apparently for insurance reasons, coaching had to be moved out of school hours. Shinty has thus come off the school curriculum. However 1996 may be an auspicious year to resolve this problem. As well as being Kyles Athletic's centenary, it is also the year in which the new Argyll and Bute Council assumes control of its school under local government reorganisation.

GAZETTEER

compiled by Rev Iain C Barclay

There are three Statistical Accounts of Scotland written in the last of the three centuries. They provide for today's reader a century by century gazetteer of every parish in Scotland. Subsequently they have become a most useful historical insight not only for historians but for any who have an interest relating to a particular area such as that of the Parish of Kilfinan, the 'home parish' of Kyles Athletic.

The first Statistical Account was the inspiration of Sir John Sinclair and was compiled between 1791 and 1796. The 'country ministers who wrote the Statistical Accounts in the seventeen eighties had seen it in personal and Christian terms.'[1] That for Kilfinan was written by the Parish Minister, the Rev M Alexander McFarlane in 1795.

The Second Statistical Account was again written by the Parish Minister, the Rev Joseph Stark in 1843 and in many ways reflected its predecessor.

In 1944 the idea of producing a Third Statistical Account developed. The publication was sponsored by the Scottish Council for Social Service and the Rev George Cairns was the author of the chapter on the Parish of Kilfinan. His contribution, originally drafted in 1951 and revised in 1955 was not published till 1961, five years after his death.

Each of those accounts have followed a pattern highlighting the principal features of the geography and the society of this 32,306 acre parish. In tracing the changes which this community has enjoyed, endured or loathed over the past 100 years, it gives a suitable template to follow for the purpose of this gazetteer.

175

The Parish itself is bounded on its western side by Loch Fyne from Ardlamont Point north to the Largiemore Burn. Thereafter it follows the burn eastwards to Cruach Moine-phuill. It then strikes south following the high points of Cruach nan Gearran, Cruach nan Tarbh, Cruach nam Broighleag to Beinn Breac and thereafter east to the Caladh Burn till the latter flows into Loch Riddon. From this point the eastern side of the Parish runs south, bounded by the West Kyle, to Ardlamont Point.

The name, Kilfinan is best rendered as the 'holy place of Finan' rather than the 'church of Finan'. It may be as the Rev George Cairns suggests in the Third Statistical Account that Finan was 'an ardent disciple of St Columba'[.2]. But as there is no evidence to support this contention and the name Finan appears in connection with other religious sites, it may be that zealous followers of Finan named the site in memory of their teacher and spiritual director. The dates which are generally suggested for the foundation of this religious site are between AD500 and 700.

With this in mind it would be useful to free ourselves from the dominant idea that all religious influences affecting the West of Scotland came from Ireland via Iona as part of the Columban mission, and this for two reasons. Firstly it is known that there was a Christian site on Iona prior to Columba. Therefore it may not have been the Finan associated with the Columban mission whose name Kilfinan now bears either because of a visit or because of a commemoration. Secondly, it is believed that in the early part of the sixth century there was evangelistic activity in south Kintyre stemming from a direct visit of a Christian mission from Ireland. Whilst it is nothing more than conjecture, it is possible that it was through this line of influence that the name Finan became associated with the local site. No matter how the question is viewed, no evidence appears to be available at present to substantiate any hypothesis as to who this local 'patron saint' may have been. But whatever else we should not view the matter as closed. Archaeology, albeit on a small scale, is still being carried out and with it there is the hope that some indications may be found which would anchor this particular Finan in 'time and space'.

Recent History

Of all that may be said about the past 100 years there must be included reference to the increased knowledge of the history of the parish resulting from archaeology. For example, V G Childe's[3] article *Chambered cairns near Kilfinan, Argyll*, Dorothy N Marshall's[4] work on McEwen's Castle published in 1983 and the most recent of which is the *Kilfinan Parish Survey Preliminary Report 1992* carried out by Glasgow University Archaeological Research Division.[5] Perhaps of the greatest significance was the publication in 1992 of the seventh volume of the report of the Royal Commission on Ancient & Historic Monuments of Scotland: Mid Argyll & Cowal.[6]

The Changing Church

Perhaps of all the things in life one of the first five in which we would wish to see no change is within the Life of the Church, whether we are members of it or not. Some may say that this has been a century of turmoil for the church, but that would be to ignore the Reformation in the sixteenth century, the Restoration in the seventeenth, the General Secession in the eighteenth and the Disruption in the nineteenth century. The church has never been that static and unchanging institution we have often sought it to be, or believed it to be and our century under review adds to that premise.

The Free Church of Scotland, emerging as the numerically stronger body from the Disruption of 1843, had by 1896 established its presence in the Parish of Kilfinan with congregations in Kilfinan, Millhouse, Kames and Tighna-bruaich. Yet it to was about to experience a disruption of its own. The Free Church, like the Church of Scotland had as its authority the Bible and as its statement of belief the Westminster Confession. But as the new 'biblical criticism' gained ground and as its advocates in the liberal wing of the church grew in number it became increasingly obvious that there was a change in the theological climate. In response to these developments, the Free Church General Assembly in 1892 passed a Declaratory Act which allowed some freedom of interpretation of the terms of the Westminster Confession of Faith. The response of the more conservative wing of the Free Church was to oppose such a course of action passion-

177

ately. An unsuccessful attempt was made in 1893 to have the Act repealed. Those in support of repeal included the Free Church Minister of Raasay, the Rev Donald McFarlane. At that time, the Free Church congregation at Millhouse and Kilfinan were without a minister of their own, and so invited Mr McFarlane to supply their pulpits in the course of his journey home from the General Assemby. His sermon swayed the members of the congregations from a general sense of accepting the Act, to one of outright opposition. In consequence these two congregations became the first to secede from the Free Church of Scotland and were subsequently joined by two ministers and 4,000 members. As a result the Free Presbyterian Church of Scotland was constituted. The denomination built its first church near Kames crossroads. Being of corrugated iron and given the passion of the district to find 'bye names' for most things let alone people, the worshippers were soon called the 'Tin Kirkers'. In 1939 it was replaced by the more permanent building juxtaposed on the same site. The Free Presbyterians in the parish represented the spiritual interest of a significant number within the population. However they experienced considerable decline during the Second World War and immediate post war years and in 1952 their last full time minister, the Rev James Tallach left for Stornoway. This decline continued to such an extent that today it may be fairly said that the cause of Free Presbyterianism in the parish has been extinguished.

Following this secession from the Free Church, the churches of Kilfinan and Millhouse were closed for worship. Neither church was replaced as the movement of the population towards Kerry had continued over the latter years of the nineteenth century and Tighnabruaich was experiencing a growth in terms of its popularity as a residential village. In response to this change the Free Church of Scotland built a new church in Kames, opening in 1894, and known initially as Kilfinan Free Church. However, within a year of its opening the union between the United Presbyterian Church and a large part of the Free Church of Scotland brought further change, when the congregation decided to leave the Free Church to become a congregation of the United Free Church of Scotland. A similar course of action was taken by Tighnabruaich Free

Church, thus bringing to an end the presence of the Free Church in the Parish of Kilfinan.

But what was happening to the 'Kirk' at this time? There had been a number of issues which had found a focus in the Disruption. One of the major issues was that of Patronage, whereby the Patron of a parish appointed the minister. This was abolished by Act of Parliament in 1874 What had perhaps been of greater importance at the time was the issue of adapting parish boundaries, 'some of which had been fixed by land tenure in the twelfth century', to the movements of population which evolved out of the industrial revolution. In the Parish of Kilfinan this movement manifested itself with the development of the gun powder works at Millhouse and the commercialisation of the inshore fishing industry.

The response of the Established Church to this issue was to build Kilbride Chapel of Ease in 1839. But the Chapel Act under which Kilbride had been built was judged null and void by the Court of Session in 1842 because of the inherent denial of the rights of the patron to present the minister. Thus Kilbride continued as in effect a mission station under the Superintendence of the Kirk Session of Kilfinan. Another development within the Established Church was the opening in 1862 of Tighnabruaich Church which was also a chapel under the authority of the Kirk Session of Kilfinan until it was erected into a quoad sacra parish on 10 March 1882.

Within this broad picture of the ecclesiastical life of the area there can be seen a great multiplicity of buildings which through the major Union of 1929 would generate a demand for rationalisation.

The Union of 1929 was brought about by the uniting of the two major strands in Scottish Church life, namely that of the Church of Scotland with a major part of the United Free Church of Scotland. Within the context of the Parish of Kilfinan the first step in this process was between Tighnabruaich Parish Church (quoad sacra) or the 'High Kirk', now called Tighnabruaich West Parish Church and Tighnabruaich United Free Church, now called Tighnabruaich East Parish Church. The congregations were united in 1931. Both buildings were retained for use until 1942 when the West became a furniture store for the belongings of those families who had been evacuated when the Ardlamont area had become a temporary restricted area to facilitate pre D Day military training. 'After the war the building was never restored to use, though a service was in fact held, less to worship the Almighty (it would appear) than to establish a legal right. Finally in 1949 it was sold to Argyll County Council and now forms part of Tighnabruaich School.'[7] Following the closure of the West, the East simply became Tighnabruaich Parish Church.

In Kerry, Kilbride Chapel of Ease had attained quoad sacra status following the abolition of the Patronage Act in 1872. It continued its connection with Kilfinan till 31 December 1956 when the link was dissolved. Thereafter it was united with Kames Parish Church on 27 January 1957 to form the parish church of Kames & Kilbride. The church at Kilbride closed in 1985.

With the link between Kilbride and Kilfinan broken a new link was forged between Kilfinan and Tighnabruaich. This continued until the union between the congregations of Kames and Kilbride and Tighnabruaich, when a new title was given, that of Kyles. Thereafter the link became that of the Parish Churches of Kilfinan with Kyles. In 1992 the church building in Tighnabruaich was closed leaving the former Kames Free Church, now Kyles Parish Church serving the eastern side of Kilfinan Parish with the Old Parish church serving the west.

Other focal pints of worship in the parish have included the monthly services at Otterferry and Ardlamont, both of which ceased prior to the Second World War. Of the other Christian denominations the Roman Catholic community worship in Tighnabruaich House and St Martins Scottish Episcopal Congregation meet in Kyles Parish Church.

There is no evidence of any other Christian denomination or group meeting for a sustained period of time within the century under review. But formal acts of worship do not constitute the only religious activity. The name of Craigengower has for years been synonymous with a restful holiday in the most beautiful surroundings of the Kyles of Bute for church groups who have come from the length and breadth of Scotland. The house was originally built for Mr Adam Black MP of Adam & Charles Black, Publishers, in 1853. Subsequently it passed into the ownership of James McDonald of the

Keppoch Branch of Clan Ranald before being gifted to the Church of Scotland in 1938. However at the end of the 1992 season the house closed preparatory to its subsequent sale and a great work of the church which had lasted for almost half a century, in various aspects, was drawn to a conclusion.

But just as not all religious activity is to be found in formal acts of worship, neither has all religious activity which has affected the parish been visible. The Parish of Kilfinan has been part of the Presbytery of Dunoon since the latter was erected by the General Assembly of the Church of Scotland on 18 December 1638.[8] In turn the Presbytery has been part of the Synod of Argyll since its inception also on 18 December 1638. Originally, it formed the Synod along with the Presbyteries of Kinloch (renamed Campbeltown), Inveraray, Kilmore (renamed Lorne) and Skye. In recent decades with the increased availability of relatively inexpensive and quick communications the place of the Synod as a tier in the Church of Scotland's ecclesiastical administration was called in question. On 31 December 1992 the Synod by now encompassing only three Presbyteries (Dunoon, South Argyll and Lorne & Mull) passed into history, ostensibly making Church administration easier by removing the middle step between Presbyteries and the General Assembly.

Population

As with many rural parishes the population is declining. In this past century the size of the community peaked in 1911 when it reached 2,709. Of the subsequent decades the decline in recent years has become less but that merely because there are fewer people domiciled in the parish. The census returns relate the downward movement; (1921), 2,199; (1931), 1,489; (1951), 1,253; (1961), 1,096; (1971), 967; (1981), 956; (1991), 844.[9]

With the growth in popularity of the area as a place for retirement there is hope that the population statistics will not drop further. That being said however there remains one missing ingredient which is required to stimulate community growth and that is employment.

Education

Just as the parish has numerous churches so it also has

181

numerous schools and just as many of the former are closed so too are the latter. The schools at Ardlamont, Millhouse, Kilfinan and Otterferry have all closed in the past 100 years leaving Tighnabruaich Primary School as the focal point for education. This school has also changed its role from providing an education for children up to the age of 15 years to being a primary only. The foundations of the former wings of the school where domestic science and woodwork were taught are all that remains of the communities last self-contained education system.

Those who wished to progress their education beyond the age of 15 years have always had to attend Dunoon Grammar School or some similar secondary school such as Kiel, originally at Southend, Kintyre but now at Helenslee, Dumbarton. Children pursuing their education in Dunoon were required to find accommodation on an individual basis, but in the 1970s a purpose built school hostel was opened for Monday to Friday residential use by the pupils. For those whose families so wish there has developed in recent years a daily bus service so allowing attendance on a day pupil basis.

The decline in the parish's population has had its effect on the number of children receiving and eligible to receive full time education. Even though the number of children had remained at the number quoted by George Cairns in his entry in the Third Statistical Account, 140, it is unlikely that given the technological advances which society has experienced since the 1950s and for which schools have had to adapt that secondary education would not require to have been centralised and therefore able to serve a wider catchment area.

But education is not confined exclusively to children. Continuing education has been and still is provided through evening classes under the auspices of the Workers Educational Association and Glasgow University Extra Mural Classes. The libraries at Tighnabruaich and Millhouse have given way to a library van which makes its rounds of the parish once in every three weeks.

Transport

Of all the areas of human life and society which have both experienced and brought change in the Parish of Kilfinan it is transport. It is of course impossible to speak of Tighnabruaich, Auchenlochan and Kames without reference to the piers and the various ships which formed part of the infrastructure of community life up and until their withdrawal from service in 1969. The pier at Tighnabruaich, which had been rebuilt and was reopened in February 1885, was always considered to be the main port of call and 'was visited by the turbine *King* or *Queen* on her way to Inveraray, McBrayne's *Columba* or *Iona* en route to and from Ardrishaig and the *Duchess of Argyll* or whatever steamer was on the Arran via Kyles run'.[10] However as a means of transport the steamer entered into serious decline in favour of the private car following the Second World War and 'by the 1950s only the *Queen Mary II* from Glasgow and McBrayne's mail steamer called daily, with the Greenock *Duchess*, Craigendoran paddlers and the Ayr excursion steamer coming alongside as their cruise schedules demanded'.[11]

Whilst steamer services as such have now passed into history Tighnabruaich pier still provides an access point for many hundreds of visitors to disembark from the PS *Waverley* or from one of Caledonian McBrayne's car ferries used in a passenger only role. Of those ferries the names *Juno* and *Jupiter* are especially note worthy as they are the third in line to bear those names sailing in the Kyles of Bute. The first was the PS *Jupiter* built and acquired in 1896 by the Glasgow & South Western Railway Co. This was followed in 1898 by her sister ship, PS *Juno*. The second series to bear those names were again paddle steamers built and acquired in 1937 for the Caledonian Steam Packet Co. Finally there are the ones presently operated by Caledonian MacBrayne on the Clyde today which were built and acquired in 1974.

But this same positive note with which Tighnabruaich pier may be spoken of cannot be struck in relation to the other piers of the area. Going south, Auchenlochan closed after the 1948 summer season and Kames after the 1928 season.

But this century has also been a time in which sea communications have opened up albeit on a some what limited scale. A steamboat pier was opened at Largiemore in 1900. Until then the Inveraray steamer ferried passengers ashore, in a procedure similar to that in use at Blindman's

Bay, serving the Ardlamont area. Despite the new pier however, passenger traffic was so light that the service ceased in 1903. MacBrayne's took up use of the facilities of the pier by extending their existing summer season only cruise to Ardrishaig to include an optional cruise across Loch Fyne. By 1914 however the pier was only used for cargo and even this service was finally terminated in 1948. But in 1993 a nostalgic trip was paid by the PS *Waverley* which came alongside at Largiemore and in so doing recaptured an era that for most present could never have been seen.

Another sea transport venture in this century was the hovercraft service to Tighnabruaich in the mid 1960s, but like the other services on the Clyde at this time, it was a relatively short lived venture. A further brief venture in the late 1970s was 'for a car ferry route across Loch Fyne to Tarbert, but in fact all that resulted was a contractor's short lived service from nearby Ardmarnock Bay using one of Caledonian Mac-Brayne's small landing craft'.[12] In some senses this was the forerunner to the opening by Caledonian MacBrayne of the public Portavadie to Tarbert vehicular ferry service in 1994.

Coupled with this, the late 1950s and early 1960s saw the emergence of the 'package holiday', initially to Spain and then to warmer climes generally. In tandem with this were the various clan societies who chartered aircraft for members to visit relatives in the United States so bringing into focus, through a holiday, family reunions which could at one time only have been dreamt about.

In the late 1940s, early 1950s the introduction of the then North of Scotland Hydro Electric Board began the public supply of electricity from Rothesay. The area covered was from Ardlamont to Otterferry though initially with the exception of Portavadie. This change was ultimately to bring about a reduction in the use of coal, as people chose the 'cleaner fuel' or when it became possible electric central heating. Thus the Clyde Puffer continued its decline from its heyday, when apart from domestic consumption, a boat load of coal per week was off loaded for the powder works alone, to today, when coal is brought to the district ready bagged for delivery.

But the most definitive change of the century must have been the 'new road' which opened in 1969. This introduced easier and more flexible access to the area for the individual or family using their own car, and to that extent it was considered an asset. But it also enabled those who wished, to shop outwith the parish. Not only did the shops themselves suffer, but the delivery vans disappeared bringing a further contraction of business life.

Local Government

Such a theme may seem out of place in a volume focusing on the centenary history of Kyles Athletic. But as the year in which the centenary is celebrated also sees the Local Government (Scotland) Act 1994 being fully implemented with the councillors elected in the Local Government elections assuming their independent role in the new unitary authority, it is perhaps fitting to pause and see where we have come from in the past 100 years.

By the end of the 19th century the local government of Scotland was run by 200 burgh councils, 33 county councils and 869 parish councils as well as by a variety of Commissions, such as Police, District Committees and Boards such as schools and roads. The first and most complete reform came with the Local Government (Scotland) Act of 1929 which abolished 'many smaller units of administration; replaced the old classification of burgh by two new classes – large and small burghs – differentiated by the extent of their power; set up district councils for the landward area of counties (ie those portions of the county not included in the burgh) to provide certain local services; and replaced the many rates hitherto levied by a consolidated county and burgh rate'.[13]

The 1929 Act which had come into effect in May 1930 was repealed and replaced, but without any modification to the structure of local government, by the Local Government (Scotland) Act of 1947.

By the 1960s however, 'it was widely felt that the structure which had by then served for over 30 years was becoming inadequate to the task'.[14] A Royal Commission was established in 1966 and three years later published its findings which were substantially accepted by the government of the day. The Local Government (Scotland) Act 1973 brought to Scotland the concept of District and Regional local government and came

185

into effect on 16 May 1975. Through this act Argyll County Council gave way to Argyll & Bute District and as a part of Strathclyde Region.

At the local level the Act instituted the Community Councils of which over 1,000 ultimately came in to being and of which Kilfinan Community Council is one. The Community Council was devised as a means of 'assessing and expressing local opinion, thus bringing to the attention of the local authorities and other public bodies any matters of concern to their particular locality'.[15] They were not to be seen as a third tier of local government and therefore do not have any statutory functions. That said, however, it was envisaged that they could, 'collaborate with local authorities and services and initiate community projects'.[16]

In local government terms this century is about to close with a further radical transition, from a two tier to a single tier form of administration. In promoting this concept various arguments were brought forward in support. It was claimed that the two tier system had led to confusion in the public mind, that duplication of function and waste despite implementing a plan of rationalisation still continued and that an element of friction could be identified between some authorities. In addition it was advocated that there should be greater opportunity for consumer choice and partnership between public sector, private sector and individual in discussing how services should be delivered. 'In particular the government pointed to such initiatives as the creation of school boards; self governing status for schools; the promotion of home ownership and the rights of tenants; the deregulation and privatisation of transport services; the impact of compulsory competitive tendering; the developing role of Scottish Enterprise, Scottish Homes and local enterprise companies; and the increasing emphasis placed on value for money in local government, strong financial management and public accountability.'[17]

Whilst there is little doubt that communities such as the Parish of Kilfinan have felt like minnows in an ocean, on a population comparison with the region (Kilfinan 1981 Census 956 compared with Strathclyde Region estimate 30 June 1983, population 2,382,077) the parish has benefited from a number of the observations made above. For example Scottish Homes was a substantial contributor to the highly successful Abbeyfield House project; Tighnabruaich Primary School has its own School Board as well as its Parent Teacher Association and Argyll Enterprise funded the development of the Kames Industrial Area.

The first election under the Local Government (Scotland) Act 1994 took place in May 1995 when those elected began to 'shadow' their post for the ensuing year. Before Kyles Athletic play their last game of the 1995/1996 season the new unitary authority of Argyll & Bute Council, encompassing Helensburgh and Luss will have taken on their responsibilities in local government.

Occupations

In reflecting upon the forms of employment which have supported the community throughout the past hundred years, the principal one is agriculture. But the ravages of change which have extinguished some occupations from the community's life and brought others from a sudden start to an abrupt end have also been experienced on the land. In W D Allen's *List of Sheep Marks for the County of Argyll*[18] we see that 34 declared marks were allocated to the farms and small holdings of the parish, with one irregular mark noted. But nearly 75 years later many of those farms no longer sustain families as independent units and the names of others have disappeared completely. For example the fields of Ardmarnoch, Auchnaskeoch, Inveryne, Melldaloch and Achrossan are now farmed as part of Craignafeoch, those of Auchdalvorie are now farmed as part of Stillaig, and those of Corra as part of Point & Kildavaig, whilst those of Drum, Kilfinan, Fearnoch, Lindsaig and Cravunachan are farmed as Otter Estate, and that of Strone as part of Ballimore Estate.

Whilst the families concerned would not be dependent on their sheep holding for their livelihood it is of interest to note that others mentioned by Allen no longer have an agricultural function; Craigengower House and Kilfinan Hotel lands no longer keep sheep

The second occupation which may be mentioned as one of significance was that of the Powder Mill at Millhouse. The

187

Millhouse works, one of three including Furnace and Glen Lean, opened in 1839 and was in continuous production until its closure in 1921 when approximately 60 jobs were lost. 'Redundancy Payments were made to all employees, based upon individual occupation and length of service. The formula used was two weeks wages for 1/5 years' service, and up to sixteen weeks' wages for 40/50 years' service, plus a proportional share of a Special Severance Bonus.'[19] The loss of such a job opportunity was a serious blow to a community whose ability to attract any form of industry was severely limited by distance, resources and a convenient market for the end product.

The Forestry Commission was similarly a key employer but began to run down their local commitment, closing the Tighnabruaich Office and ultimately centralising the area administration at Blairmore. The late 1970s early 1980s represented a significant period of change within forestry especially with the sale of woodland for investment purposes and the advent of the private forestry management companies who represent the owners' interest. As an example of this change two of the afforested areas in the parish, the 3,173 acres of the Ardmarnock Forest and the smaller 372 acre Caladh Woodland are at the time of writing, being offered for sale. Generally the attractiveness of woodland as an investment vehicle comes in the fact that the timber income generated from commercial forests is free from Income Tax. Furthermore, there is 100% relief with regard to Inheritance Tax, as well as a low exposure to capital Gains Tax.

Ardmarnock Forest was mainly developed in the decade 1960-1970. Sitka Spruce is the dominant planting, with Scots, Corsican and Lodgepole Pines, Japanese Larch and various broad-leaved species also being represented. Caladh Woodland is more diverse, with its main planting period ranging from 1957 to 1960.

The most recent and perhaps the singularly most dramatic and short lived source of employment within the parish was the ill-fated platform site at Portavadie. This site was developed under the auspices of Sea Platform Construction (Scotland) Ltd who received government approval to proceed with development on 9 January 1975. The development was to be a platform site with a workers' village on the field called Pollphail. When built the, 'Great Hole, six fathoms deep at the seaward end, and extended out to the six fathom mark, with a huge metal coffer dam, filled with sand, keeping out the sea, was never used. Pollphail also was never occupied, and after a few years began to deteriorate rapidly.'[20]

But any community in Scotland which enjoys the beauty of the hills, the convenience of access by sea and is close to a major centre of population is likely to be a focus for holidays. In more recent times we have become accustomed to any activity which generates income on a broad scale as being referred to as an 'industry'. It is however doubtful if the hotels, boarding houses and landladies offering hospitality in a wide range from full board to 'room with service' would ever have referred to it by that term. But whilst this 'industry' may not have created many 'steady jobs', the holiday visitors did, and continue to generate much needed income across a wide range of related services which in turn generated work for those whose employment did not relate to the seasonal migration 'doon the watter'.

As has been mentioned above the pattern began to change in the late 1950s and as lore would have us believe, was finally dealt a mortal blow through the take up of all available accommodation during the building of the Portavadie platform basin in the 1970s. Visitors were unable to find accommodation and sought alternative areas in which to holiday. When the work on the Portavadie site ceased and the village accommodation became available to the holiday market, the regulars had in many cases found alternatives which captured their imagination as once the Kyles had done. The 'tide' had finally turned.

With the passage of time we all suffer from viewing the past with rose tinted spectacles and seeing things as being much better than they actually were. In our mind we see crowds milling off the steamers and Simpson's and McBride's taxis whisking them away to their holiday accommodation. But did so many people actually holiday in the Kyles? 'The 1921 census for certain parts of the region were abnormally inflated by summer visitors. The excess was most apparent in Oban, North Knapdale, Kilfinan and Inverchaolain, but these

189

places except North Knapdale were excluded from the analysis.'[21] It seems our spectacles are not always rose tinted!

Whilst fewer holiday in the area than once did, the holiday community, whether casual visitors, holiday home owners, students at the Sailing School or those who have an interest in boats, sailing or fishing, remains a vital element within a fragile local economy and outwith agriculture provides the largest number of employment opportunities, albeit many on a part time basis.

Sports and Pastimes

This seems an almost pointless sub-heading when this volume is focused on the centenary of Kyles Athletic. Other sports have been rumoured to exist. Some have been sufficiently foolhardy to play football on the shinty pitch, fortunately outwith the latter's fixture list! Yet strangely enough for all the enthusiasm which crept in the late eighties, early nineties for this 'alternative sport' it failed to rival the historical enthusiasm for shinty. It must of course be noted that another great issue of the latter part of the century has brought a change to the game – the place of women in sport. As shinty is part of the school's sports curriculum at primary level it is also played by girls who have been critical of the fact, that on leaving the Kyles to pursue secondary education at Dunoon Grammar, they also leave the Camanain behind!

[1] Drummond & Bulloch 'The Church in Victorian Scotland' 1843-1874 p80
[2] Third Statistical Account, p.316
[3] Childe; V G 'Chambered cairns near Kilfinan, Argyll' *Proc Soc Antiq Scot* 66 1931-1932 pp415-420
[4] Marshall; D N 'Excavations at McEwen's Castle, Argyll in 1968-69' *GAJ* x 1983 pp131-142
[5] Atkinson, Driscoll & Watson 'Kilfinan Parish Survey Preliminary Report 1992' 1993 Glasgow
[6] RCAHMS 'Argyll: an inventory of monuments' Volume 7 (Mid Argyll & Cowal) 1992 HMSO
[7] Cross; D G 'A Church History of the Parish of Kilfinan' 1963 unpublished typescript p41
[8] 'Fasti Ecclesiae Scoticanae' Volume 4 1923 Edinburgh
[9] Census Reports, Registrar General for Scotland Edinburgh

[10] Inverclyde District Library 'Clyde Piers: a pictorial history' 1982 Greenock p56

[11] ibid. p56

[12] ibid. p59

[13] Scottish Information Office 'Local Government in Scotland' Fact sheet 28 1984 p3

[14] Himsworth; C M G, 'Local Government (Scotland) Act' 1994 1995 Edinburgh p39-8

[15] Scottish Information Office ibid. p13

[16] ibid. p13

[17] Himsworth ibid. p39-9

[18] Allen; W D 'List of Sheep Marks for the County of Argyll' pp. 35-40

[19] McConnell; K J 'The story of Kames/Millhouse Gunpowder Works' in 'Kilfinan: walks, history, reminiscences' ed. H F Torbet 1984 Privately printed p66

[20] Torbet; H F 'The Portavadie Platform Site' in 'Kilfinan: walks, history, reminiscences' ed. H F Torbet 1984 Privately printed p67

[21] Darling; F F 'West Highland Survey' 1955 OUP p114

Kyles Athletic 1996
back – *Kenny Macdonald, Donald Macrae, Peter Mobeck, Neil Nicolson,*
    David Taylor, Ali Wren, Peter Currie, Tam Whyte
front – *Fraser Macdonald, Ronnie MacVicar, Andy Macdonald,*
    Iain Macrae